The Emperor's Table

ISBN: 978-81-7436-453-1

© Roli & Janssen BV 2008
Published in India by
Roli Books in arrangement with Roli & Janssen BV, The Netherlands
M-75, Greater Kailash-II Market, New Delhi 110 048, India.
Phone: 91-11-29212271, 29212782, Fax: 91-11-29217185
Email: info@rolibooks.com; Website: rolibooks.com

Editor: Neeta Datta
Design: Sneha Pamneja, Mukesh Singh
Layout: Narendra Shahi, Nabanita Das
Production: Kumar Raman, Naresh Nigam

Printed and bound in Singapore

The Emperor's Table

THE ART OF MUGHAL CUISINE

SALMA HUSAIN

FOREWORD
PAVAN K VARMA

Lustre Press
Roli Books

❦

TO MY PARENTS QASIM AND MARIAM AJMERI
WHO GAVE ME THE APTITUDE FOR WRITING

❦

Contents

Shah Jahan's ancestors: Humayun, Babur, Jahangir, and Akbar; Mughal,
18th century; British Library.

Foreword

Salma Husain's book on Mughal cuisine is an appetizing effort. It not only traces the history of the Mughal emperors vis-à-vis their fondness for food and contribution to the growth of recipes, but is an engaging read on the role of each ruler's personal likes and dislikes as well as how this has shaped the course of food habits in India.

The history and growth of cuisine is an intangible heritage that has been prone to loss over time. In fact, cuisine is an essential aspect of our culture. We draw our food habits from the terrain we inhabit, our seasons and our festivals. Our food is, therefore, intricately linked to our daily lives.

Mughal cuisine in India owes its birth to the country's Islamic past. The Muslims brought their rich gastronomic history to India and this influence is now an inextricable part of our food culture. In fact, Mughal cuisine is a fragrant blend of our Indo-Islamic past and the Ganga-Yamuni *tehzeeb* that characterizes us. Hence, it contains elements that are common to both the Hindus and the Muslims and reflects, essentially, a fusion of cultures, and the meld of common ingredients to create something new and innovative. This history is interesting, both from an intellectual point of view as well as a human one, to observe how our lives and our cuisine began to reflect and record the changes that were seen in society. In these times, the importance of following the development of how the dishes and food habits have changed over time is equally vital to the study of society and its inhabitants.

This book is also an important document in that it helps to retrieve the idea of specialization that was so inherent to cooking in India in the early days. Today, fast food has taken over our lives. Though all of us probably enjoy burgers and chips as much as indigenous recipes, there can be no doubt that the skill and devotion that any Indian recipe requires was an art form in its own right. It was the same relish that made meal times a significant aspect of our lives before the bite-and-type culture took over. This book highlights the role that food played in people's lives and how, in turn, people affected its growth. The ethos that each dish reflected, therefore, traces the history of a nation, its people and its changing cultures.

The painstaking research that has gone into the volume is praiseworthy. But, perhaps, the author has left the tastiest morsels for the end. Each chapter on a Mughal emperor is accompanied by some mouth-watering recipes, lucidly explained and easy to attempt. They certainly manage to revive the aroma and flavour of the royal days gone by and encourage us to enjoy their whiff once again.

I would like to felicitate Salma Husain for an important book on a significant aspect of our culture and history.

— **Pavan K Varma**

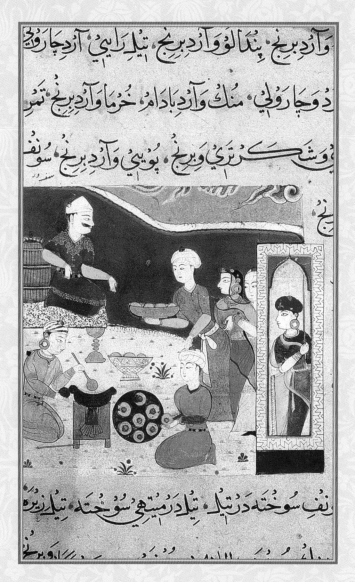

Sultan of Mandu directing the preparations of sweets, Pre-Mughal,
Nimatnama, c.1490-1510, National Museum of India.

Author's Note

This book contains tables of the seven Mughal emperors who ruled India from 1483-1858 and took culinary art to its zenith. The Mughals definitely changed the food scenario. These rulers, from Central Asia, swept through civilization and shaped the unpredictable course of history. It is said that their army rode with a sword in one hand and salted meat in their saddle.

I have tried to give authenticity to the recipes by undertaking extensive research on the subject and going through manuscripts of medieval India in different libraries and museums. Most of the recipes included here have been selected from the original Persian manuscripts and also printed books of relevant period. However, the recipes have been modified to an extent to suit the modern times.

A visit was made to Ferghana, home town of Babur, to collect old recipes of the valley. A careful review of the recipes from the *Ain-i-Akbari*, a manual of Akbar's time, a selection from *Alwan-e-Nemat* and *Nuskha-e-Shahjahani*, Persian manuscripts containing royal recipes of Jahangir and Shah Jahan's kitchens, and study of an Urdu book called *Buhadur Shah ka Ahde-Hakoomat* has given authenticity to the recipes. It is unfortunate that recipes of games and birds, which remained favourite of the Mughal emperors, could not be included as present days restriction prohibits their availability. Some of the spices not available then have been included to make dishes tastier. Use of dried fruits, saffron, and ghee has been reduced considerably. I hope you enjoy the royal recipes of the emperors who have left a legacy of food behind them, besides their monuments and gardens.

I would like to thank Dr Naseem Akhtar, in charge manuscript section, National Museum of India; Khalid Kamal Faruqi, librarian Jamia Hamdard, who permitted me to use the library extensively; Janab Mufti Sahib and Ram Niwas, staff of the library, for their tireless help in providing help for my research. I am equally grateful to Chef Taj Mohammad and Jagdish Das who tried all the recipes of the book with me. I am also grateful to Mr Sadruddin of the Uzbek embassy for his valuable help in checking the recipes collected from Uzbekistan and permitting me to watch a master chef cook the wedding pulao.

My sincere thanks to Ram Niwas who typed the manuscript several times, without his help this book would not have taken shape. Lastly, my most sincere thanks to Chef Manjit S Gill of Welcomgroup who in spite of his busy schedule spent time to improve the recipes, and also to Major S S H Rehman, Executive Director ITC Ltd., my mentor, who encouraged me to carry on research in this field. My sincere thanks to Mr Pavan Varma, Director General, ICCR, for writing the foreword of this book. I would like to thank Late Mr Rabindra Seth whom I approached every second day to discuss the book and returned with fresh ideas and energy to complete the book.

My thanks to Pramod Kapoor, Publisher Roli Books; Neeta Datta and Amit Aggarwal for their support in bringing out this book.

The Mughal Dynasty Tree

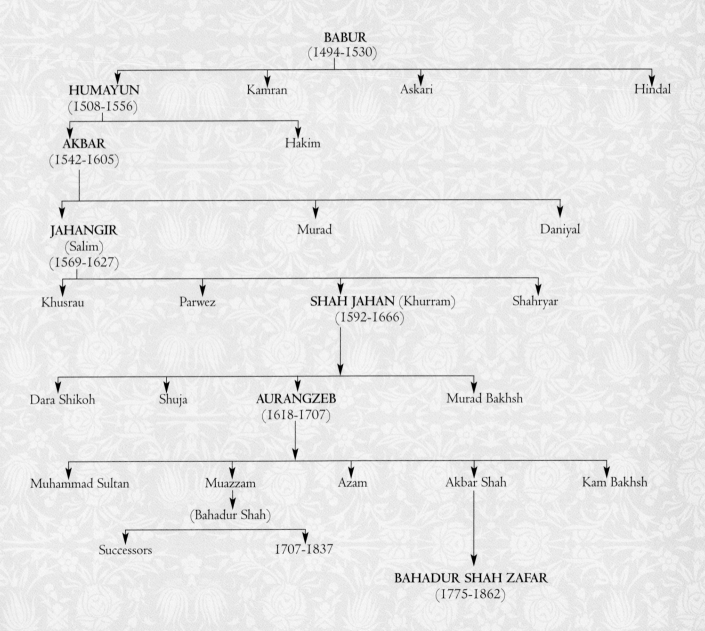

BABUR
(1494-1530)

HUMAYUN
(1508-1556)   Kamran   Askari   Hindal

AKBAR   Hakim
(1542-1605)

JAHANGIR   Murad   Daniyal
(Salim)
(1569-1627)

Khusrau   Parwez   SHAH JAHAN (Khurram)   Shahryar
(1592-1666)

Dara Shikoh   Shuja   AURANGZEB   Murad Bakhsh
(1618-1707)

Muhammad Sultan   Muazzam   Azam   Akbar Shah   Kam Bakhsh

(Bahadur Shah)

Successors   1707-1837

BAHADUR SHAH ZAFAR
(1775-1862)

Babur

Humayun

Akbar

Jahangir

Shah Jahan

Aurangzeb

Bahadur Shah Zafar

A feast attended by Uzbek, Hindu and Qizilbash envoys who brought gifts and money to Babur; Mughal, c.1590; British Library.

Introduction

During the sixteenth and seventeenth century the splendour and opulence of the Mughal courts were at its zenith — the like of which had not been seen in over a thousand years. Between 1626 and 1712 the Mughal emperors, Turks by origin but with Mongol, Persian and Hindu blood in their veins, ruled the greater parts of the Indian subcontinent The Mughals came from Central Asia, which was the cultural cauldron of three classical civilizations of the world — India, China and Greece. Cities like Bukhara, Samarqand, and Herat were great centres of wealth and sophistication.

The Mughals, who had an overwhelming impact on literature, music, painting, and architecture, also revolutionized the culinary arts. They combined indigenous traditions with their Persian-influenced culture, refining it to please the eyes as well as the palate. Skillful at projecting imperial wealth and power, the Mughal emperors used sophisticated dining to impress their courtiers, subjects, and foreign visitors.

They delighted in the beauty of art and nature and tried to develop and improve what pleased them. The Mughal emperors were also multi-talented and rich in cultural accomplishments. Each one of them had a different quality and together they made a strong, beautiful empire. Babur was the man of fine literary taste; he was an author, calligrapher, and also a composer of poetry. Humayun inherited his father's talent in the field of poetry and also had an interest in mathematics, astronomy, and astrology. Akbar was a keen philosopher and was skilled in the art of architecture. Jahangir was a naturalist and a landscaper, known for his gardens; he also had a great authority on paintings. Shah Jahan excelled in architecture. Besides being a connoisseur of gems and jewels, he was also devoted to music and dance. It is believed that he himself was a good singer. Aurangzeb did not patronize any of the fine arts except calligraphy. He had some interesting architecture but nothing remarkable to leave a mark on the pages of history.

It is a well-established fact that the Mughal emperors influenced both style and substance of Indian food. They turned simple Indian cooking into an art and patronized the art with passion. Their hospitality remains legendary. Among the Mughal emperors after Babur his grandson, Akbar, took a personal interest in the royal kitchen. He devised rules for the conduct of the kitchen staff and appointed high-ranking officers to administer the territory.

Cooking opens doors to many cultures and creeds. Geography also plays an important role. Central Asia, from where the Mughals came and from where the famous silk route started, has a rich tradition and an instinct culture with a history of many centuries. Their respectful relations with their neighbours like Tajiks, Kirghis and Tatars, Turkemans, Ukrainians, Russians, Armenians, and Azerbaijans have greatly influenced the Uzbek region. The Mughals brought all these influences with them and gave Hindustan a rich and varied cuisine.

The advent of the Muslim rule between the tenth and eleventh centuries resulted in a great fusion of culinary traditions. With Indian, Persian, and Middle Eastern cuisine, culinary art reached the peak of sophistication. Mughals have left behind a legacy of food, which remains alive even now after centuries.

All the Mughal emperors except Humayun were hardworking people. They worked tirelessly but also had time for leisure. The distinction between their work and play was ambiguous. Akbar played polo to assess the character and spirit of his imperial officers. Hunting was a warm up for battles. The pomp and magnificence of their lifestyle was an essential display of the grandeur

Emperor on hunting ground; Mughal, 18th century;
National Museum of India.

and an expression of their power that brought distance between the subject and the emperor. This inspired awe and devotion in them and made them loyal.

'The Mughal imperial capital was a movable city,' says Bernier, a French traveller, 'when they travel they take with them, like our gypsies, the whole of their families, goods, and chattels. The capital and the court were wherever the emperor happened to be at that moment. True to their Central Asian heritage, the Mughal emperors were often on the move and as the emperor moved so did the entire panoply of court… in duplicate.'

As mentioned earlier, the Mughals were gourmets and food was important to them, so when the Emperor moved, the first to move was their kitchen. 'It is the custom of the court,' says Manucci, an Italian traveller, 'to move the royal kitchen ten o clock at night prior to emperor's departure to ensure that royal breakfast is prepared by the time the emperor arrives next morning.… It consist of 50 camels, who carried the supplies, 50 well-fed cows to provide milk, 200 coolies to carry China and other serving dishes, a number of mules to carry cookwares, also there are dainties in charge of cooks (from each only one dish is expected) sealed in Malacca velvet. A military contingent escorted the royal kitchen with water-bearers, sweepers, leather workers, and torchbearers.'

The *Ain-i-Akbari*, a gazetteer of the Mughal empire, detailing every aspect of Akbar's government written by his courtier Abul Fazl has a vivid and fascinating chapter devoted to the imperial kitchen. Abul Fazl provides a list of recipes of some of the dishes which reflect that Mughal diet heavily relied on rice, wheat, gram, barley, and some other lentils. Bernier describes how the shops were stacked with pots of ghee, rice, wheat, and endless variety of other grains. The Central Asian and Persian influence is evident in the recipes listed in the *Ain-i-Akbari*. Abul Fazl writes that the kitchen department was headed by Mir Baqawal (master of the kitchen), an officer of the rank of 600 horses (in Akbar's reign). Hakim Humam held the post under the direct control of the *vizier* (prime minister). Mir Baqawal had under him an army of cooks, tasters, attendants, bearers, and a special officer for betel. The cooks came from Persia, Central Asia, Afghanistan, and from different regions of India. *Hakim* (physician) of repute assisted in the preparation of the daily menu keeping in mind the temperament of the emperor and the nutritive value of the food served to him. Many recipes were given by the royal hakim as a remedy for indigestion, stomachache, to produce lustful feelings and increase vitality of the emperor. These recipes made with medicinal properties sharpened the intellect, made the eyes shine, gave a glow to the skin, and improved hearing.

The hand written account of the royal kitchens of the Mughal emperors reveals that very few spices like cumin, coriander, ginger, pepper, cinnamon, cloves, fennel were used in cooking. Cartloads of almonds, pistachios, walnut, dried apricots and plums, and raisins were imported to Hindustan along the new roads which were constructed to facilitate trade throughout northern India, Central Asia, and Persia. Nuts and raisins were added to the dishes to make them exotic and befitting for the imperial table. The use of sugar and saffron with lemon juice was common almost for every dish, perhaps, to create the sweet and sour effect of Persia and to reduce the heat of the saffron which was used in large quantity. Almond was used not only to give body to the dish, but also enrich the flavour and give strength to mind and body.

The royal kitchen had its own budget and a separate account department. In the beginning of the year, the sub-treasurer made out an annual estimate and received the amount. Every month a statement of the expenditure was drawn and submitted to the *vizier*. Every day 1000 rupees was disbursed for the expense of the king's table.

Provisions for the royal kitchen were collected from various parts of the empire without regards to cost. Fruits from Kabul, ducks, water fowls and certain vegetables were obtained from Kashmir, and water from River Ganges. Sheep, goats and fowls were maintained by the kitchen and were given special diet mixed with aromatic herbs, silver, gold, pearls, saffron marbles mixed with sugar, perfumed grass to get pleasant-smelling flesh from the animals to suit the royal palate. Cows were fed with cotton seeds, sugarcane, nutmeg, coconut, cinnamon, pulses, partridge eggs, and bamboo leaves besides perfumed green grass. They were never kept for less than a month. Rice came from Bharaij, Gwalior, Rajori and Nimlah, and ghee from Hissar. Food was flavoured by using aromatic herbs. Perfumes were made and developed by *hakim* by mixing fragrant flowers and leaves, like of sweet orange, bitter orange, mango, lime, sweet basil, and many more.

Food was cooked in almond oil, lard obtained from the melted down fatty tail of sheep, apricot oil, and oil from the seed of grapes. Ghee was coloured differently with saffron, spinach, and turmeric and was flavoured with rose water musk and other perfumes. Water for the use of emperor and the harem was perfumed with camphor, rose petals, sour orange leaves, sweet orange leaves, and fennel leaves. Spices were used for seasoning and to add aromatic shade to the cuisine. Popular spices were cumin, black pepper, coriander, fresh ginger, and fennel. Herbs like mint, coriander, and dill were in use but with the passage of time the spice box became richer with many more spices.

Trappings of birds on the banks of the River Baron, near Kabul; Akbar-Mughal c.1598; National Museum of India.

The Mughal emperors were by nature meat eaters; perhaps, the climate of Central Asia and the hunting habit needed them to be strong. Hunting was also their lifestyle as it kept them fit and well trained for battles. The meat was associated with strength and valor. Kings and rulers were expected to excel as warriors and hunters and also to display the strong sexual powers with their numerous wives and concubines. They also had an important task to deal with the burden of government.

Lamb was the most favoured meat, besides games and birds. Under the guidance of *shahi hakim* (the royal physician), the expert cooks of the imperial kitchen prepared meat dishes which were light and digestible. The use of gold and silver as well as pearls and other precious stones were used in cooking, as per their medicinal values. Fish was made odour-free by applying the paste of fresh lime leaves, cardamom, cloves, lemon juice, and salt, and was kept overnight and then cooked with great skill so as not to leave any bone behind. Similarly birds of prey were slaughtered and treated for cooking. Sandalwood paste was applied on them to remove unpleasant odour. They hunted even while moving and thus the smoked and grilled and barbecued meat adorned their table. Birds and animal of prey were stuffed with rice, dried fruit and eggs to make a wholesome food while marching. Later this style of cooking was given a sophisticated touch.

An area was demarked close to the royal kitchen where vegetables, enjoyed by the emperor, were grown with special care. The vegetable beds were watered with rose water and musk to get a special aroma.

The *Ain-i-Akbari* describes three classes of cooked dishes. *Sufiyana*: consumed on Akbar's days of abstinence, no meat was used and the dishes were those made of rice (*sheer biranj, zard biranj, khushka,* and *khichdi*), wheat (*chikhi*, essentially the gluten of wheat isolated by washing and then seasoned), dals, spinach, and a few other leafy vegetables, as well as *halwas,* sherbats, etc. The second class comprised those in which both rice and meat or wheat and meat were combined (pulao, *shulla, shorba, haleem, harees, kashk,* and *qutab*); the third class was that in which meat was cooked in ghee, spices, yoghurt, and eggs to create dishes like *yakhni,* kebabs, *dopiyazah, musamman, dum pukht,* and *malghuba*. This system of food continued throughout the Mughal domain but with the passage of time, many more classes were added to them.

It is interesting to note that Akbar the great not only adopted blending of religion and cast in his administrative policies but his table was also a true mirror of this amalgamation, which included Indian dishes besides Turkish and Persian food which he had inherited from his ancestors.

The Mughals did not pay much attention to the adornment of dining place; their food itself was always rich, colourful and decorated with gold and silver leaves. Each cook tried his best to excel and present something unique. Some items of food were made to look like gems and jewels, fruits were cut in the shape of flowers and leaves, dried fruits was glazed with Babool gum and added to pulaos, and ghee for cooking was coloured and flavoured. Yoghurt was set in seven colours but in one bowl, and cottage cheese was set in bamboo baskets. Colouring and garnishing of food reached a new height during Jahangir's reign as Nurjahan was artistic and brought sophistication to the royal table.

A great variety of food was prepared every day for the emperor to choose from and some dishes were kept half done, so that they could be served immediately should the emperor ask for them.

Rice ground to flour then boiled and sweetened with candy sugar and rose water was eaten cold — perhaps, this is where the present-day *kheer* (rice pudding) has come from. The flour of rice mingled with almonds made as small as they could and with some fleshy parts of chicken stewed with it, and then beaten into pieces, mixed with sugar and rose water, scented with amber was a popular dessert of the royal table. Dishes made into cakes of several forms of the finest wheat mingled with almonds and sugar candy, some scented and some not, filled with fruit jellies also adorned the royal *dastarkhwan*. Various kinds of pickles, chutneys, fresh ginger, lemons, and various greens in bags bearing a seal of Mir Baqawal, saucers of yoghurt piled up were also included in the royal menu. Pickles had medicinal value; it is learnt that the pickles made

with fruit sharpened the appetite and hunger, ward off illness, and also helped in digestion. Breads made with finest wheat flour were round, white and light.

Except in banquets, which were regular features of the court, the emperors ate alone in the privacy of their harem. No outsider has ever seen any emperor while dining, except once when Friar Sebastien Manriquea, a Portuguese priest, was smuggled by a eunuch inside the harem to watch Shah Jahan eating his food with Asaf Khan, Nur Jahan's brother. Food was eaten on the floor. Sheets made of leather and covered with white calico protected the expensive Persian carpets. This was called *dastarkhwan*. It was customary for the king to set aside a portion of food for the poor before eating. The emperor began and ended his meals with prayers.

Hunting game: Black buck with does; Akbar-Mughal, c.1598; National Museum of India.

Chewing of betel (*paan*) finds numerous references in the Mughal culture. It was an important ingredient to end the meal. The emperor was given the *bira* of betel after he had washed his hands. The betel leaves were rubbed with camphor and rose water. Eleven leaves made one *bira*. The betel nut (*supari*) was boiled in sandalwood juice. Lime was mixed with saffron and rose water. Chewing of betel leaf (*tambul*) had many qualities.

It made the tongue soft, the mouth sweet-smelling and ward off flatulence. Betel nut is a laxative; and lime removes bitter and sweet phlegm.

Though Islam prohibits drinking of alcohol, the Mughal emperors specially Babur, Humayun, and Jahangir indulged in it and had a strong attraction for wine. According to the Jesuit Father Monsterrate, who was one of the three members of the first Jesuit mission to Akbar's court, said that Akbar rarely drank wine as he preferred *bhang*. Shah Jahan was temperate and Aurangzeb abstemious. Jahanara Begum, daughter of Shah Jahan, was extremely fond of wine; they were imported from Persia, Kabul, and Kashmir.

Tobacco and huqqa, the ubiquitous symbols of princely India in later times, was known in the Mughal courts in the seventeenth century. Tobacco was introduced in the Deccan by the Portuguese in the second half of the seventeenth century. A story mentioned by Abraham Eraley, in his book makes an interesting reading. He writes that a court historian of Akbar's court, Asad Beg, during his mission to the Deccan towards the close of Akbar's reign chanced upon it and carried a bag on his return to Agra. He presented some of the tobacco in a jewelled betel bag to the emperor along with a jewelled studded huqqa on a silver tray. Akbar was curious and asked to prepare a smoke, when the pipe was ready and Akbar took it, the *shahi hakim* approached and forbade his doing, but Akbar smoked it to gratify Asad Beg. He then summoned other *hakim* to the court and sought their advice on tobacco smoking. He was told that they have no knowledge on the subject, as it is a new invention. Akbar passed the pipe to other nobles of the court who enjoyed it thoroughly

and thus the habit caught on. Jahangir disliked tobacco and banned its smoking. *Ulemas* issued *fatwas* against it saying tobacco smoking was an innovation and not sanctioned by the religion, but all this had little effect on people and tobacco smoking became widespread and a common feature of royal household. It is interesting to note that duty on tobacco was the major source of income for the empire.

One of Babur's main disappointment with India was that there were no good fruits. He made efforts to cultivate sweet grapes, melons, and pineapples in Hindustan. Akbar set up a royal orchard and employed horticulturists from Central Asia and Persia. Their fondness for fruits made them take steps to grow fruits in the soil of Hindustan. To encourage farmers, horticulture was exempted from tax. They enjoyed mangoes. Babur was not particularly fond of them but Jahangir, Shah Jahan, and Aurangzeb found the fruit best in flavour and taste. This emphasized that the Mughal emperors were Indian at heart.

Bernier records that the Mughal emperors as well as their nobles consumed vast quantity of fruits both fresh and dried. The shops in Delhi were well stocked with nuts and dried fruits such as almonds, pistachios, walnut, raisins, prunes, and apricots from Persia, Balkh, Bukhara, and Samarqand. In winter, fresh grapes, black and white, brought from the same countries wrapped in cotton, pears and apples of three to four kinds, and melons were eaten, stewed or raw, and preserved in sugar and nuts. They were called *murrabas* and their use was advised by the *shahi hakim*. In summer, mangoes were plentiful and cheap. Best mangoes came from Golconda, Bengal, and Goa. Bernier also saw many *mithai* (sweetmeat) shops, but was not impressed with them, firstly they were not well made, and secondly, they were exposed to dust and flies.

Drinking water was a major item of expense in the royal household, for the Mughal emperors were fastidious about water and normally drank only from River Ganges, which had to be brought from considerable distance. Akbar called it water of immortality. The water was brought in sealed jars. A special department called *Aabdar-Khana* was in charge of water supply to the royal household, experienced water tasters were a regular unit of royal entourage and also accompanied emperors on hunting. For cooking, water from River Yamuna and Chenab was mixed with little water from the River Ganges or even rain water was collected and stored in the kitchen. In early part of Akbar's reign, water was cooled with saltpeter.

In the later part of the Mughal era, with the arrival of Portuguese, potatoes and chillies were added to the food list. Excellently well-dressed potatoes, or potatoes cooked in several ways were added to the royal meals in the post-Jahangir period. Shah Jahan's table had rich spicy food besides different kinds of *qormas*, *qaliyas*, breads, kebabs, and pulaos, a lot of Indian and some European delights also made their appearance on the royal *dastarkhwan*. With the passage of time, the royal table became more and more Indian absorbing the local and regional spices and flavours. Dishes like *poori*, *paratha*, *khandvi*, *kachori*, and many

more savouries and sweets became part of the emperor's *khasa*. In turn Indian cuisine also got enriched with foreign influences, the sweet and sour taste, dried fruits, aromatic herbs, perfumes, and saffron.

The most lavish table was that of Bahadur Shah Zafar. His table had every cuisine – Turkish, Persian, Afghani, and Indian – kebabs of venison, partridge and fish, *booranis*, *samosas*, *khandvi*, *dals*, *salans*, and a variety of pulaos and sweetmeats. He enjoyed eating *besan ki roti* with *rahat jani chutney*, lamb *qorma*, and *dal padshah pasand*.

All these details show how far the Mughal emperors had developed the art of cooking clearly to satisfy refined and gastronomical concerns. They have left behind not only the accounts of their rule in India, but also the exotic dishes and their style of cooking like *dum pukht* (which is now being popularized by ITC Hotels, who are also pioneer in their efforts to revive the old dishes). The style set the standard for others to follow, so that even with the decline of the empire after 1707, rich cuisine continued to evolve at the courts of the Nizams of Hyderabad, the Nawabs of Lucknow, Murshidabad, Rampur, and among the rulers of Rajasthan and Kashmir. Today in Pakistan and India, the legacy of the Mughals is reflected in the grand and luxurious food served at formal banquets.

The names of the emperors and their queens linked with dishes make an interesting part of the menu in many five-star hotels and even wayside restaurants. Poor Mughals little did they not know that they would be remembered with *qormas* and pulaos besides the Red Fort and Taj Mahal!

Culinary Terms and Techniques Used

You may be familiar with some of the culinary styles but the ones which specifically lend Mughlai cuisine its distinctive touch are described below:

Dhungar: This is quick smoke procedure used to flavour meat dishes, *dals* or even *raita*. The smoke very effectively permeates every grain of the ingredients and imparts a subtle aroma, which enhances the quality of the dish. The procedure may be carried out either at the intermediate or at the final stage of cooking. This is a common technique employed while making kebabs. The method is as follows:

In a shallow utensil (*lagan*) in which the meat or mince has been marinated, a small bay is made in the centre and a bowl or onion skin or even betel leaf (depending on the dish) is placed. In it a piece of live coal is placed and hot ghee, mixed with aromatic herbs or spices, is poured over it and covered immediately with a lid to prevent the smoke from escaping. The coal is then removed from the utensil and the meat put through further cooking process.

Dum: Literally means breath and the process involves placing the semi-cooked ingredients in a pot, sealing the pot with flour dough and applying very slow charcoal fire from the top, by placing some live charcoal on the lid and some below. The Persian influence is most evident in this method though in India it has acquired its own distinctive character. The magic of *dum* is the excellent aroma, flavour, and texture which results from slow cooking. This method is followed for a number of delicacies such as *shab deg*, pulao, and biryani. Any dish cooked by this method is called *dum pukht*.

Galavat: Refers to the use of softening agents such as raw papaya or any souring agent to break the fibers of meat and tenderize it.

Baghar: This is a method of tempering a dish with hot oil or ghee and spices. It may be done either at the beginning of the cooking as in curries, or at the end as for pulses. In the former, the fat is heated to smoking point and after reducing the flame, spices are added to it. When they begin to crackle, the other ingredients are added. The same process is carried out in a ladle which is immersed in the cooked dish and immediately covered with a lid, so that the essence and the aroma of the spices, drawn out by hot ghee are retained in the dish giving it their flavour.

Tandoor: Tandoor is a clay oven in which food is cooked on the spit. Indian spitted foods require frequent basting, for the meat is never larded.

Seekh kebabs are minced meat croquettes shaped with the hand over an iron skewer, or *seekh*, to the thickness of a pencil. The layer of meat is thin, and fierce heat, usually a charcoal or wood fire, cooks these kebabs in a minute or so.

Boti kebabs are also made on the skewer. Small pieces of very tender meat are marinated for several hours and then cooked under intense heat, basted with butter. The marinade forms a glaze on the surface.

Kofta is minced meat shaped into small balls then braised in *qorma* style, curried, or even spitted on small skewers. Some koftas are formed over sweet sour plums, or a paste of minced dried apricots and herbs; some are moulded on eggs and these are called *nargisi* (narcissus). The meat itself is finely grounded then blended or pounded to force meat. Herbs, seasonings and spices are added, and sometimes cream or yoghurt or egg is used to bind.

Moin: It is shortening of dough. In this process fat is rubbed into the flour and made into a dough for *kachori, poori* or *paratha*. This makes the product crisp, flaky and crumbly.

Yakhni: The cuts for *yakhni* are generally bony pieces with flesh on them. These cuts are usually taken from the joints and the ribs of the animal and cooked with onion, crushed coriander, ginger, garlic, garam masala, and water to acquire stock. The basic purpose of meat in preparing *yakhni* is to derive the juice and flavour and hence the shape of the meat does not count much. *Yakhni* is stock made of meat, vegetables, and spices and is used for cooking rice. In Kashmir, there is a meat preparation made with yoghurt and dried ginger powder which is also called *yakhni*.

Techniques and Utensils Used

A brief account of the Mughal emperors and their cooking ethos has been given in earlier pages. It remains to consider the ways in which the food was cooked, and in what kind of utensils it was cooked and served.

Heat for cooking was provided by wood fire, which was burnt in open *chulha*. The *chulha* was made with clay to suit the size of the cauldron. All the food was cooked on either direct or indirect heat and fire was controlled with handmade fans and by arranging burning wood or coal under, above or on the sides of the cooking pot. Abul Fazl records that Akbar's kitchen consumed 100,650 maunds of firewood in a year.

Several cooking operations were in use: drying, parboiling and cooking in water, seasoning, frying, dry roasting, grilling, smoking, and steaming. The sealing of the pot and cooking on low heat called *dum pukht* was prevalent then, mostly in hunting grounds where the animal of prey was cleaned, washed and buried in underground pit to be cooked. The material to be cooked was wrapped in leaves. The pit was then closed with a slab of stone and charcoal placed on top. Cooking for a prolonged period over low heat had its own virtues, sealing of the pit with stone slab or mouth of the pan with dough enhanced the taste of the food as food was cooked in its own juices and no aroma was allowed to escape. Though the style was practiced in India earlier, but it received impetus as a Muslim refinement.

Drying of meat was prevalent as long distances had to be crossed while marching and at times hunting was not possible. Meat was cut, minced, dried and filled in the intestines of the animals, thrown on the saddles and carried while marching. This was an easy way to carry food for the marching army; wherever need arose and halt was ordered the load was brought down, cut into pieces, grilled on open fire and consumed. It was wholesome and nutritious for the tired soldiers; it is, perhaps, the beginning of the sausages, which we have today.

Steaming was common, though there were no steamers like today but the use of technique to achieve steaming in simpler way was adopted by the cook. The material to be steamed was tied in a muslin cloth and placed over a wide-mouthed vessel in which water was boiled.

Kebabs were grilled on open grills on charcoal, and also on hot stone slabs. The meat was skewered on wooden skewers or on the branches of pomegranate or figs. The wooden skewers and branches of trees were soaked in water for a few hours, dried in the sun and then used for grilling. This prevented the bamboo skewers from getting burnt.

The food was cooked in gold, silver, copper (copper pots were tinned before use), stone, and earthen pots. It is interesting to note that the cooking vessel in which the meal was made influenced the food cooked in it, and the effect that it exerted on the general health of the emperor is worth mentioning. For example, cooking of rice in a copper pot destroyed gas, removed spleen disease, and was recommended by the *hakim*. Rice cooked in bronze destroyed all three humors. Rice cooked in gold alleviated poisons, ward off indigestion, jaundice, diseases caused by wind besides enhancing vigor, vitality and eroticism. Rice cooked in silver vessel removed phlegm, biliousness, and indigestion. Rice made in tinned vessel rendered the body cool, and in earthen pot reduced biliousness. The earthen pots made from the earth from dry land were good for blood, skin, and healing of wounds. Similarly, other metals had their own effect, their use was explained and advised by the *hakim* and followed by Mir Baqawal, who communicated it to the cooks. Fish was always made in earthenware. This luxurious way of serving and preparing food continued until the time of Shah Jahan as Aurangzeb, being a simple man, did not believe in luxury. Bahadur

Shah Zafar had very little time to enjoy, but whatever little time he had he did indulge in fine living and courtly etiquette.

Not only the way of cooking, but also the way food was served is interesting to note. Food was served in dishes made of gold and silver studded with precious stones; use of fine China, and dishes of precious stones like ruby, turquoise and jade was also common as it detected the poison immediately by changing its colour. Great precaution was taken to ensure the purity of the dishes served to the emperors. Mir Baqawal on a piece of paper made a list of vessels and dishes sent inside the harem with his seal and ensured that none was changed. Baqawal, the cooks, and other servants carried the dishes and mace-bearers preceded and followed to prevent people from approaching them. In short, all precautions were taken to safeguard the royal *khasa* on its journey from the kitchen to the royal harem where the emperor awaited to enjoy it.

Babur hunting deer between Ali Shang and Alangar, near Kabul;
Mughal, c.1590; British Library.

Babur
(1494-1530)

NAME	ZAHIR-UD-DIN MUHAMMAD
TITLE	BABUR
BORN AT	FERGHANA
DATE OF BIRTH	FEBRUARY 14, 1483
DATE OF CORONATION	APRIL 22, 1526, DELHI
ZODIAC SIGN	AQUARIUS
DIED ON	DECEMBER 26, 1530
BURIED AT	AGRA

Sultan Said Khan and Baba Khan Sultan paying homage to Babur near Ferghana;
Mughal, Baburnama, c.1597-98; National Museum of India.

Babur, born on February 14, 1483 at Ferghana in Transoxiana, modern Uzbekistan and Tajikistan, was a scion of the dynasty that had reigned undisputed throughout eastern Iran and Central Asia since the time of its progenitor Amir Timur. He was named Zahir-ud-din Muhammad (Defender of the Faith) but that was a tongue twister for the rustics of Ferghana, so they nicknamed him Babur (tiger which proved fitting).

In 1495, at the age of 12, Babur became the ruler of Ferghana after the sudden death of his father, Umar Sheikh Mirza. It was a shaky throne. Babur survived for a short time with the help of his maternal grandmother, Aisan-daulat Begum, and was driven away from his homeland by Shaibani Khan, a descendant of Chenghez Khan who had made it his mission to extirpate the Timurids from Central Asia.

Driven from his homeland, he spent a lifetime winning and losing kingdoms. He, finally, reached the Indian subcontinent, where he defeated Ibrahim Lodi in the Battle of Panipat and on April 22, 1526, in Delhi, public prayers were offered in the name of the new Emperor of Hindustan, Zahir-ud-din Muhammad Babur.

Babur then marched to Agra after covering a distance of 280 km from Panipat. He reached on May 4, at the height of summer and made it his capital city. His decision to stay back in Hindustan was an unpleasant surprise for his men. They had expected him to return to Kabul with the booty. The climate of India oppressed them and powerful adversaries were marching from all sides to suppress Babur.

Babur regarded his Indian conquest with qualified enthusiasm. His active and inquisitive mind found much to investigate and wonder at in India, especially the flora and fauna, but the country had little appeal as he mentions in his memoirs. Babur had a mission to accomplish, as he writes in his memoirs, 'India is a large country: masses of gold and silver, and workmen of every profession, trade innumerable and without end.' Besides material reward, he also wanted the prospects of glory that would be his, and a place in history as the founder of an empire, as he himself said:

'Give me but fame, and if I die I am contented
If fame be mine, let death claim my body.'

Babur's decision to make India his home brought him several allies. During the first two years of his reign, he was so generous and kind that terror and dread banished from the hearts of all men. He was 43 years old and he knew that India had to be conquered, inch by inch. The immediate danger was from the Rajputs, under Rana Sanga, who were preparing to march against him. Babur was worried as his men were not only gloomy at the extended stay in Hindustan but also further demoralized by the Rajput reputation of valour. Babur in a dramatic gesture revived the loosing spirits of his men. In this hour of crisis, he decided to return to obedience to win divine favour and to gain the moral authority, to declare war against Rana Sanga, he unleashed the martial fury of his men. He faced his men and raising his arm to invoke the blessing of Allah ceremonially took the pledge to renounce wine. In a very theatrical manner he called for his abundant stock of wine, poured all the ruby-red liquor on the ground in front of his aghast troop, smashed his goblets of silver and gold and gave away the fragments to the poor. He also vowed not to trim his beard thereafter. The plan was perfect. The mood of the army swung dramatically and fire filled into each heart. The battle

Banquet being prepared for Babur and the Mirzas; Mughal, c.1590; British Library.

against Rana Sanga was won. Such was the promptness of his actions, which he always displayed in his military exploits.

This victory left him in undisputed control of the centre of Hindustan. Now he extended his boundaries by the simple device of granting his men tracts of lands, which were not yet conquered, and sending them off to claim their own. His empire extended from the Himalayas in the north to Gwalior in the south, and from Punjab in the west to the frontiers of Bengal in the east. He would have extended his empire further but death did not permit him to do so.

He toured throughout his kingdom to study the internal problems of the country, and to make his administration easy he divided his kingdom into fiefs and assigned them to his officers. He also introduced express letter mail between Agra and Delhi. His permanent place in history rests upon his Indian conquests, which opened the way for imperial line.

Soldier of fortune as he was, Babur was not the less a man of fine literary taste. He was an acclaimed writer and poet and wrote in Persian and Turkish. In thick of his difficulties, he found leisure in writing and composing verses. He had a curious notion that literature had healing powers, writing irrelevant poetry caused illness. Babur has several books to his credit, prose and poetry, a treatise on jurisprudence, and an interesting book on prosody called *Mufassil*, a Persian collection of *masnavis* called *Mubin* which had a large circulation in his days. But his best-known work is his biography *Baburnama*, a classic in its genre. He wrote his memoirs in chaghatay Turkish, Abdur Rahim Khan-e-Khanan translated it into Persian and presented it to Akbar in 1589. This book is the most precious treasure of Indian historical literature. It reveals Babur in his true colours and gives a vivid account of his countrymen, their appearances, hobbies, tastes, and pursuits. It contains a detailed account of his visits to various places in his kingdom, their physical features, flora and fauna, works of arts, and industry.

Apart from the books, Babur had to his credit several other cultural accomplishments such as musical compositions and a creation of a new and distinctive style of calligraphy called Baburi. His greatest passion outside literature was gardening; one of his first projects was to build a garden complex. He was a keen horticulturist. He introduced grapes and melons in the Garden of Eight Paradises in Agra.

The capacity of Babur to find joy in so many things kept him alive in difficult days. Whatever he did was a vigorous and cheerful expression of his own self. Babur delighted in being Babur. He always said: *Babur be aish kush keh alam dubara neest* (enjoy the luxuries of life Babur, for the world is not going to be had a second time).

Babur was a man of simple taste which reflected his nomadic pattern of life. He did not enjoy the food of Hindustan and found the cooks unreliable after the attempt to poison him at Tuglaqabad. The only food he enjoyed in Hindustan was fish else he remained alien to Indian food. He lamented the fact that this country had no ice or cooked food in the bazaars. He loved food of his country, relished Turkish delights, and enjoyed the dishes of Kabul. He also missed the fruits of his country like musk-melons, grapes, and apricots. It is to be noted that the old Turkish food was not sophisticated and exotic, it was simple and wholesome. Turkish food became exotic during the Ottoman Empire. Fresh vegetables and fruits, meat mixed with cereals, roasted sheep, and rice flavoured with saffron

were found on his table. He missed the breads of Samarkand and Bukhara.

Babur ruled India for less than five years, but inaugurated a Mughal era of unparallel splendor when great cities, palaces, mosques, gardens, and monuments were built. He and his successors came to be known as the Grand Mughals, celebrated for their florid manners and courtesies, the display of their hospitality, and their delight in material comforts.

When his iron will began to falter, he resorted to wine. He was not in good health and took little interest in government. He often went into depression and wanted to become a hermit. He was tired of ruling and reigning and wanted to give away his kingdom to his son, Humayun. On December 26, Babur passed away and was laid to rest in the Garden of Eight Paradises in Agra, now renamed Aram Bagh. Around 1543, during the reign of Sher Shah, the mortal remains of Babur were transferred to Kabul and buried in his favourite garden on the Shah-i-Kabul hill in a simple grave. The man of mountain was back home.

STEAMED LAMB SAVOURY
Manty

PREPARATION TIME: 1 HR. • COOKING TIME: 40 MIN. • SERVES: 4

Ingredients

Wholewheat flour (*atta*)	1 cup / 200 gm / 7 oz	Lamb mince	300 gm / 11 oz
Salt to taste		Salt to taste	
Egg yolk	1	Black peppercorns (*sabut kali mirch*), freshly	
Vegetable oil	1 tsp / 5 ml	ground, to taste	
For the filling:		Pumpkin (*sitaphal*), grated	2 tbsp / 30 gm / 1 oz
Ghee	¼ cup / 55 gm / 1¾ oz	Garlic (*lasan*) paste	¼ tsp
Onion, finely chopped	1	Yoghurt (*dahi*), whisked	½ cup / 110 gm / 3¼ oz

Method

1. Knead a hard dough with wholewheat flour, salt, egg yolk, and water. Add oil and knead again; cover and keep aside for 30 minutes.
2. Divide the dough into 12 equal portions. Roll each portion out into a thin sheet and cut into 12x12 cm squares.
3. **For the filling**, heat the ghee in a pan; add onion and sauté. Add lamb mince, salt and black pepper powder; stir-fry until the moisture evaporates. Add pumpkin and mix well. Cook for 10 minutes on low heat until the lamb is cooked and the moisture evaporates.
4. Place a portion of the lamb mixture into the centre of a square, fold up the sides and seal the ends. Steam the squares for 35-40 minutes or shallow-fry in a pan till golden brown.
5. Serve with yoghurt mixed with garlic paste; sprinkle freshly crushed black pepper or sour cream.

Note: *In Uzbekistan* manty *is steamed in special frying pan called* kashkan.

STUFFED CABBAGE ROLLS
Karam Dulma

PREPARATION TIME: 30 MIN. • COOKING TIME: 30 MIN. • SERVES: 4

Ingredients

Cabbage (*bandh gobi*)	1	Salt to taste	
Lamb, boneless	500 gm / 1.1 lb	Black pepper (*kali mirch*) powder	a pinch
Onion, chopped	1	Rice	¼ cup / 50 gm / 1¾ oz
Tomatoes, sliced	2	Mint (*pudina*), chopped	1 tbsp / 4 gm
Egg	1	Lamb stock	1 cup / 300 ml / 10 fl oz

Method

1. Mince the lamb with onion, juice from sliced tomatoes, egg, salt, and black pepper powder.
2. Cook the rice until half done.
3. In a bowl, combine the lamb mixture, cooked rice, and mint; mix well.
4. Place head of cabbage in a large pot with boiling water. Blanch for about 5 minutes, remove from pot and arrange individual leaves on the work surface.
5. Put a fair amount of the meat filling on each leaf and roll up.
6. Arrange the rolls in a wide-mouthed pan, pour the lamb stock, cover and stew for about 20 minutes. Serve hot.

Yar Husain, son of Darya Khan, seeking audience of Babur at Kabul; Mughal;
National Museum of India.

RICE AND LAMB SOUP
Mastava

PREPARATION TIME: 25 MIN. • COOKING TIME: 1 HR. • SERVES: 4

Ingredients

Lamb with bones, washed, cut into cubes	500 gm / 1.1 lb	Carrots (*gajar*), large, peeled, cut into cubes	2
Rice	¾ cup / 150 gm / 5 oz	Turnip (*shalgam*), peeled, cut into cubes	1
Vegetable oil	¼ cup / 55 ml / 1¾ fl oz	Potato, large, peeled, cut into cubes	1
Onion, big, sliced	1	Salt to taste	
Tomatoes, sliced	3	Black pepper (*kali mirch*) powder to taste	
		Sour cream	2 tbsp / 30 gm / 1 fl oz

Method

1. Heat the oil in a pan to smoking point; add onion and sauté till light pink. Add tomatoes and sauté on high heat for a minute. Add lamb and cook until brown.
2. Add carrots and turnip, reduce heat to medium and stir-fry until the vegetables are soft.
3. Add 8 cups water, increase heat and bring water to the boil.
4. Add potato and rice; cook covered on low heat for 25 minutes until rice and potato are done. Add salt and black pepper powder; mix well.
5. Serve in bowls topped with sour cream.

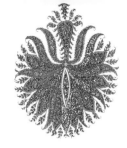

SLOW COOKED RICE WITH LAMB AND DRIED FRUITS
Mevali Palov

PREPARATION TIME: 20 MIN. • COOKING TIME: 1 HR. • SERVES: 4

Ingredients

Rice, washed, soaked for 15 minutes		Sour cherries, destoned	1½ cups
drained	2 cups / 400 gm / 14 oz	Walnuts (*akhrot*), chopped ½ cup / 60 gm / 2 oz	
Ghee	½ cup / 110 gm / 3¼ oz	Currants (*sultana*) ¼ cup / 35 gm / 1¼ oz	
Onion, small, chopped	1	Dried apricots (*khoobani*)	½ cup
Lamb, boneless	250 gm / 9 oz	Salt and black pepper (*kali mirch*) powder to taste	
Lamb stock	2 cups / 600 ml / 20 fl oz	Refined flour (*maida*) ½ cup / 60 gm / 2 oz	
Cinnamon (*dalchini*), ground	½ tsp / 2½ gm	Egg	1

Method

1. Heat half the ghee in a pan; add the onion and sauté. Add lamb and fry until lightly brown. Add 1 cup lamb stock and cook on medium heat until half done.
2. Add cinnamon powder, sour cherries, walnuts, currants, dried apricots, salt and black pepper powder, and remaining lamb stock; cook till lamb is tender. Remove and keep aside.
3. Parboil the rice in water flavoured with rose water. Keep aside.
4. In a bowl, mix the flour and egg together and make a dough. Roll into a flat cake.
5. Melt 1 tbsp ghee in a pan; place the flour cake and spread some rice (keep one cup aside). Pour the remaining hot ghee over the rice, Cover the pan with a cloth, place the lid and cook on *dum* (see p. 20).
6. Colour the reserved rice with saffron.
7. While serving, pile the rice on a serving dish, make a border with saffron rice, and spread the lamb mixture on top.

Babur feasting in the company of Qizilbash, Uzbek and Hindu envoys; Mughal, c.1598;
National Museum of India.

Babur holding court, Mughal, 18th century;
National Museum of India.

UZBEK GARLIC PULAO

Lasan Palov

PREPARATION TIME: 1 HR. 30 MIN. • COOKING TIME: 40 MIN. • SERVES: 4

Ingredients

Rice, long grain, parboiled	2 cups / 400 gm / 14 oz	Black peppercorns (*sabut kali mirch*), powdered	1 tsp / 4 gm
Garlic (*lasan*)	1 pod	Coriander (*dhaniya*) powder	2 tbsp / 15 gm
Olive oil	1 tsp / 5 ml	Cumin (*jeera*) powder	2 tbsp / 15 gm
Vegetable oil	½ cup / 110 ml / 3¼ fl oz	Carrots (*gajar*), large, grated	6
Leg of lamb, cubed	400 gm / 14 oz	Vegetable or lamb stock	4 cups / 1.2 lt
Onions, large, thinly sliced	2	Barberries, washed, drained	½ cup

Method

1. Sprinkle olive oil on top of garlic pod and wrap in foil. Roast the garlic pod in a medium-hot oven (180°C / 350°F) for about an hour. The garlic flesh should be soft and brownish when done.

2. Heat the oil in a pan; fry the lamb cubes until nicely browned. Remove and keep aside, covered.

3. In the same oil, fry the onions until soft and light brown. Add the ground spices and mix well for 1 minute. Add the carrots and cook for 3 more minutes or until carrots are soft. Add the reserved meat and mix.

4. Add rice and lamb or vegetable stock or water (but it should be hot not cold as this would stop the cooking for a good 10 minutes). Cover and simmer on medium heat for about 10-15 minutes. Turn frequently to make sure that the rice does not stick to the bottom. When the rice is cooked through, add the barberries, remove the lid and wait until all the liquid has evaporated, turning the rice regularly.

5. Serve piping hot with a garlic head for each guest.

SPICY WHOLEWHEAT BAKED BREAD
Kyulcha

Ingredients

Wholewheat flour (*atta*)	2 cups / 400 gm / 14 oz	Coriander (*dhaniya*) seeds	½ tsp / 1 gm
Ghee, melted	1 cup / 220 gm / 8 oz	Green cardamom (*choti elaichi*)	4
Egg yolks	2	Cinnamon (*dalchini*) powder	½ tsp / 2½ gm
Yeast	1 tbsp	Poppy (*khus khus*) seeds	2 tsp / 6 gm
Sugar, powdered	¼ cup / 30 gm / 1 oz	Saffron (*kesar*), dissolved	
Salt to taste		in milk	½ tsp

Method

1. In a bowl, mix the wholewheat flour with ½ cup ghee, one egg yolk, yeast, sugar, and salt together. Knead to make a dough. Cover with a wet cloth and leave in a warm place to rise for 20 minutes. Remove the cloth when the dough doubles in volume.
2. Pound the coriander seeds and green cardamom and add to dough along with cinnamon powder.
3. In a bowl, whisk the remaining egg yolk.
4. Divide the dough into 8 equal portions. Roll the portions into small discs, coat the top with egg yolk, sprinkle some poppy seeds and bake in the tandoor for 15 minutes or in the oven at 180°C / 350°F for 15 minutes.
5. Before serving, sprinkle some saffron mixture on the baked bread.

RICE PUDDING GARNISHED WITH DRIED FRUITS
Moughli

Ingredients

Rice, broken, soaked for 15 minutes,	Walnuts (*akhrot*), coarsely chopped,
drained — ¾ cup / 150 gm / 5 oz	soaked in cold water — ½ cup / 60 gm / 2 oz
Sugar — ½ cup / 100 gm / 3¼ oz	Pistachios (*pista*), blanched, peeled,
Black cumin (*shah jeera*) powder — 1 tbsp / 7½ gm	cut into slivers — ¼ cup / 35 gm / 1¼ oz
Cinnamon (*dalchini*) powder — ¼ tbsp	Green cardamom (*choti elaichi*) powder — ¼ tsp
Milk — 2½ cups / 600 ml / 20 fl oz	Rose petals (*gulab pankhuri*)
Pine nuts (*chilgoza*), soaked in cold water — ¼ cup	for garnishing — a few

Method

1. Combine rice, sugar, black cumin powder, and cinnamon powder with milk and cook on medium heat, stirring continuously, with a wooden spoon. Bring to the boil, lower heat and cook, stirring continuously, for 10 minutes or until rice is soft and the milk has evaporated. Mix well.

2. Drain the walnuts and pine nuts and keep aside.

3. Pour the mixture into a flat dish, and serve garnished with pistachio slivers, pine nuts, and walnuts. Sprinkle green cardamom powder and fresh rose petals.

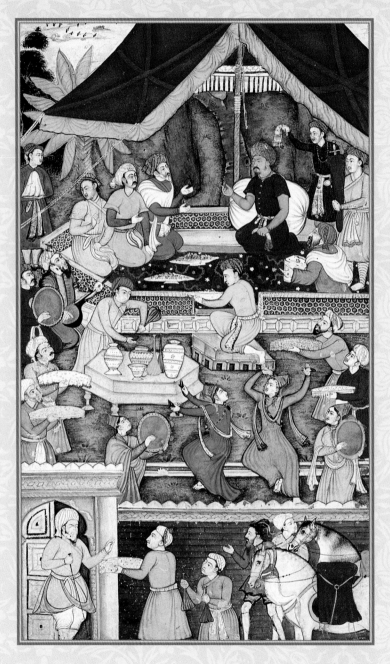

Babur camping out in the open, surrounded by men of literary tastes; Mughal, c.1598;
National Museum of India.

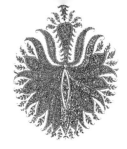

MEAT KOFTAS DRAPED IN THICK GRAVY
Riza Kjufta

PREPARATION TIME: 45 MIN. • COOKING TIME: 1 HR. • SERVES: 4

Ingredients

Lamb, leg piece	500 gm / 1.1 lb		Lamb stock	2 cups / 600 ml / 20 fl oz
Onions, medium-sized, chopped	3		Dried apricots (*khoobani*), destoned	½ cup
Salt and black pepper (*kali mirch*) powder to taste			Dried plums (*alubukhara*), destoned	¼ cup
Ghee	2 cups / 450 gm / 1 lb		Sugar	½ tsp
Tomato purée	½ cup / 120 gm / 4 oz		Black peppercorns (*sabut kali mirch*), crushed	½ tsp / 2 gm
Almond (*badam*) paste	½ cup / 60 gm / 2 oz		Mint (*pudina*) and basil (*tulsi*), chopped	
Pistachios (*pista*), blanched	½ cup / 35 gm / 1¼ oz		for garnishing	

Method

1. Mince the lamb with 1 chopped onion, salt and black pepper powder. Divide the mince into 16 equal balls.

2. Heat the ghee in a pan; deep-fry the balls until golden brown. Remove and keep the koftas aside.

3. Remove the ghee from the pan, leaving 4 tbsp behind. Heat the ghee and sauté the remaining onions until transparent. Add tomato purée and stir. Add almond paste and pistachios; simmer for a minute.

4. Add the lamb stock, dried apricots and plums, sugar, and black pepper powder; cook on low heat until the apricots and plums are soft and the sauce is thick.

5. Add the koftas to the gravy and simmer for a minute. Remove from heat and serve garnished with mint and basil.

*Celebrations in honour of the birth of Humayun in the Chahar Bagh
of Kabul; Mughal, c.1590; British Library.*

Humayun
(1508-1556)

NAME	HUMAYUN
TITLE	NASIR-UD-DIN MUHAMMAD
BORN AT	KABUL
DATE OF BIRTH	MARCH 6, 1508
DATE OF CORONATION	DECEMBER 28, 1530
ZODIAC SIGN	PISCES
DIED ON	FEBRUARY 22, 1556
BURIED AT	DELHI

Humayun, the beloved son of Babur, ascended the throne amidst great festivities under the title Nasir-ud-din Muhammad Humayun two days before the end of the year 1530. The new king was not destined to enjoy a peaceful reign, as he himself created his own difficulties and also because his rival, Sher Shah, outmatched him in diplomacy.

Humayun was not strong enough to consolidate what his father had conquered. His leniency was his mistake and his inconsistency was his blunder. The political condition of India, at the time of his accession, was miserable. The leading nobles and military rulers who had been granted large *jagirs* turned against him and plotted against him to push their own men. His brothers cheated him and tried to acquire power. Sher Khan, who after his victory at Chausa to the east of Benaras, had crowned himself king under the title of Sher Shah, inflicted a sharp defeat on Humayun at Kannauj, and expelled him from India.

Court dancers, Mughal, 18th century; National Museum of India.

After his defeat at Kannauj, he sought help from Shah of Persia and took himself out of the Mughal political arena altogether. The Shah regarded Humayun as an honoured guest. After a leisurely stay of over a year, Humayun reluctantly set out homeward. With the help of Shah Tahmasp of Persia, Humayun acquired the kingdom of Kandhar and then having disposed off his rivals he turned his attention to the reconquest of Hindustan. He advanced towards India early in the year 1555 and occupied Lahore. Humayun then entered his old capital, in triumphant procession, and ruled India for a brief span of 12 months. In Delhi, Humayun relaxed, and the remainder of his life was spent in ease and enjoyment. On February 22, 1556, he died after a fall from his library stairs.

He was married to Hamida Bano Begum, daughter of Shaikh Ali Akbar Jami, who was Prince Hindal's teacher and advisor. It took Humayun a month to convince her to marry him. She was just 14 years old when she married Humayun, who was 33. Fortune smiled on Humayun after the birth of his great son, Akbar.

Humayun had acquired proficiency in arts and science in his early years. He was very fond of poetry and had great skill in that art. In astronomy he was adept, and in geography a perfect master. Farishta says he fitted up seven halls of reception and dedicated them to the seven planets. Judges, ambassadors, poets, and travellers were received in the Hall of Moon; commanders and other military officers in the Hall of Mars; civil officers in the Hall of Mercury; gens de letters in the Hall of Jupiter, and musicians in the Hall of Venus.

The Persian craftsmen, especially the painters of the exquisite miniatures, fascinated Humayun. He was delighted when some of them followed him to Hindustan after he had regained his throne. They helped to found the Mughal school of miniature painting. In short, Humayun was gifted with those accomplishments and graces, which are highly prized in good and fashionable societies.

Hunting game: Floricans, sand grouses, saras cranes, Akbar-Mughal, c.1598; National Museum of India.

He ordered *najjars* (carpenters) to construct four boats, each of these boat had an arch, two storey high. When these boats were put together the four arches positioned opposite to one another, formed an octagonal fountain within them, which presented a picturesque view. These boats were floated on the River Jamuna and were provided with bazaars and shops. Often the emperor sailed in them from Firozabad, Delhi, to Agra with his courtiers. There were such bazaars afloat on the Jamuna that one could have whatever one liked. Gardeners made moving gardens on the surface of the River Jamuna. Various parts of this wooden structure were so skillfully joined that it looked like one with no joints. The stairs could be folded and unfolded. He also made a moving bridge.

Humayun was a great bibliophile. In spite of the fact that he was occupied in a fatal contest with a host of enemies, he managed to spare time for studies. Unfortunately, he had no time to contribute towards culture and cuisine. The earlier period of his life went in fighting and later he had very little time to do anything. His time spent in Persia and the lavish hospitality of the Shah made him favour the Persian cuisine. As Hamida herself was of Persian origin it was befitting to find Persian cuisine on the royal table of the Emperor. The Persian dishes replaced the Central Asian and old Turkish flavours. The table was now more rich and varied. Though there were the same stuffed and roasted sheep, spit-roasted chicken with herbs, koftas of different kinds, lamb cooked in tandoor but a certain amount of sophistication entered the royal kitchen. Use of nuts and saffron increased. Persian cooks excelled in the art of making sweetmeats, vegetables, and lentils, and birds were cooked in the most unimaginable ways. Sometimes there was an all white menu to please the royal palate, which was named *Jashn-e-Mehtabi*.

Humayun's life was eventful, but unromantic. As Lane-pool says, '. . . . Humayun stumbled out of life as he had stumbled through.'

A vizier delivers the petition of Mir Musavir to Humayun; Mughal, c.1555-70; National Museum of India.

Humayun with his army in a battle near Ambala; Mughal, c.1598;
National Museum of India.

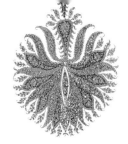

ORANGE FLAVOURED CHICKEN PULAO
Shirin Palov

PREPARATION TIME: 30 MIN. • COOKING TIME: 45 MIN. • SERVES: 4

Ingredients

Rice, parboiled in rose water with	
½ tsp saffron 2 cups / 400 gm / 14 oz	
Chicken, cut into 8 pieces 1 (800 gm / 28 oz)	
Orange peel, chopped, blanched,	
drained ¼ cup	
Ghee 1½ cups / 330 gm / 12 oz	
Carrots (*gajar*), grated ½ cup	

Almonds (*badam*) ¼ cup / 30 gm / 1 oz
Sugar 2 tbsp / 24 gm
Saffron (*kesar*) ½ tsp
Pistachios (*pista*), pounded ¼ cup / 35 gm / 1¼ oz
Onion, quartered 1
Salt to taste
Silver leaves (*varq*) 4

Method

1. Heat ½ cup ghee on medium heat in a pan; sauté the carrots until soft but not brown. Add orange peel, almonds, sugar, and saffron; reduce heat to low, stir until sugar dissolves, cover and simmer for 5-7 minutes. Add pistachios and cook for 2 minutes. Remove.
2. Heat the remaining ghee in a pan; fry the chicken to golden brown. Remove and drain the excess oil on absorbent kitchen towels; sprinkle salt.
3. Remove the extra ghee from the pan, return the chicken pieces to the pan, add onion and 3 cups of warm water; bring to the boil on medium heat. Reduce heat, cover and simmer until the chicken is tender and the moisture evaporates. Remove from heat and keep aside.
4. Layer a thick-bottomed pan with parboiled rice and carrot mixture. Then pour 1 tbsp hot ghee and seal the pan. Cook on *dum* (see p. 20).
5. Spread the rice on a platter, arrange the chicken on the top, spread some more rice over the chicken, sprinkle pistachios and decorate with silver leaves.

YOGHURT SOUP LACED WITH SAFFRON
Eshkaneh Shirazi

PREPARATION TIME: 15 MIN. • COOKING TIME: 30 MIN. • SERVES: 4

Ingredients

Yoghurt (*dahi*), whisked	I cup / 225 gm / 8 oz	Walnuts (*akhrot*),	
Butter	2 tbsp / 30 gm / I oz	coarsely chopped	½ cup / 60 gm / 2 oz
Onion, chopped	I	Salt and black pepper (*kali mirch*)	
Refined flour (*maida*)	2 tbsp / 20 gm	powder to taste	
Spinach (*palak*), chopped	I tbsp	Saffron (*kesar*)	½ tsp

Method

1. Melt the butter in a pan; sauté the onion on medium heat to light brown. Add flour and cook on low heat, until well blended.

2. Add spinach, walnuts, and 2 cups water; mix well. Add another 2½ cups water and stir constantly, increase heat to high. Season with salt and black pepper powder and bring to the boil. Lower heat and simmer covered until the liquid has thickened slightly. Remove the pan from the heat.

3. Add whisked yoghurt, spoon by spoon, to the soup and stir until well blended. Return the pan to the heat and cook on medium heat, stirring continuously, until the liquid starts boiling. Remove from heat, sprinkle saffron and serve.

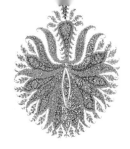

LAMB KEBABS WRAPPED IN BREAD
Luleh Kebab

PREPARATION TIME: 30 MIN. • COOKING TIME: 20 MIN. • SERVES: 4

Ingredients

Lamb, boneless	750 gm / 26 oz	Salt to taste	
Kid fat	50 gm / 1¾ oz	Black pepper (*kali mirch*) powder to taste	
Onions, medium-sized	3	Juice of lemons (*nimbu*)	2
Basil (*tulsi*) leaves	1 tbsp / 2 gm	Naan-i-tunak (see p. 56)	1
Green coriander (*hara dhaniya*), chopped	1 tbsp / 4 gm	Pomegranate (*anar*) seeds, fresh	½ cup
Spring onions (*hara pyaz*), chopped	3	Cucumber (*khira*), sliced	2

Method

1. Mince the lamb with kid fat, onions, basil leaves, green coriander, spring onions, salt and black pepper powder until a fine silky paste is achieved. Cover with a cloth. Refrigerate for 20 minutes.

2. On greased flat skewers, shape the mince as sausages. Grill over charcoal fire till evenly brown. Remove from the skewers and sprinkle lemon juice.

3. Serve the kebabs wrapped in *naan-i-tunak* with pomegranate seeds and cucumber slices.

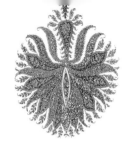

EGGPLANT OMELET SERVED WITH YOGHURT
Kukuye Bademjan

PREPARATION TIME: 10 MIN. • COOKING TIME: 15 MIN. • SERVES: 4

Ingredients

Eggplants (*baingan*), washed, peeled, cut into large cubes	500 gm / 1.1 lb
Vegetable oil	½ cup / 110 ml / 3¼ fl oz
Spring onions (*hara pyaz*), chopped	2
Eggs	6
Salt to taste	
Black peppercorns (*sabut kali mirch*), freshly ground, to taste	
Ghee	1 tbsp / 15 gm
Yoghurt (*dahi*), for serving	

Method

1. Heat the oil in a pan; add the eggplants and fry on medium heat until brown and tender. Remove and transfer into a bowl, mash with a fork and add spring onions. Leave aside to cool.
2. Beat the eggs in a bowl; stir in salt and black pepper powder and whisk well. Add the mashed eggplant.
3. Grease the frying pan with ghee; pour in the egg mixture and cook on medium heat until firm and lightly brown, gently flip the egg and cook until the other side is also lightly brown.
4. Remove onto a serving plate, cut into wedges and serve with whisked yoghurt.

DUCK GLAZED WITH POMEGRANATE JUICE
Khoresh Fesenjan

PREPARATION TIME: 15 MIN. • COOKING TIME: 2 HRS. 30 MIN. • SERVES: 4

Ingredients

Duck, small, washed, fat removed from cavity, wiped dry with paper towel	1	Pomegranate (*anar*) juice	2 cups / 600 ml / 20 fl oz
Salt to taste		Brown sugar	1 tbsp / 12 gm
Black peppercorns (*sabut kali mirch*), freshly ground, to taste		Cinnamon (*dalchini*) powder	½ tsp
		Chicken stock	2 cups / 600 ml / 20 fl oz
Ghee	1½ tbsp / 22 gm	Lemon (*nimbu*) juice	1
Onion, finely chopped	1	**For serving:**	
Walnuts (*akhrot*), finely chopped	1 cup / 120 gm / 4 oz	Walnuts, coarsely chopped	½ cup / 60 gm / 2 oz
		Pomegranate seeds, fresh	2

Method

1. Truss the duck and rub salt and black pepper powder all over.
2. Heat 1 tbsp ghee in a large, heavy pan; brown the duck on all sides on medium heat. Remove and keep aside. Drain off the excess fat.
3. Add the remaining ghee and gently fry the onion until transparent. Add walnuts, pomegranate juice, brown sugar, and cinnamon powder; bring to the boil. Reduce heat.
4. Return the duck to the pan and spoon the sauce over it. Add chicken stock, cover and simmer gently for 2-2½ hours or until tender, occasionally basting while cooking. Adjust seasoning, adding lemon juice, if pomegranate juice lacks tartness.
5. Transfer the duck onto a platter and keep hot. Skim excess oil from sauce and return to the boil. Spoon the sauce over the duck and garnish with walnuts. Add a dash of colour with pomegranate seeds. Cut the duck into four potions and serve with steamed rice.

The Royal Humayun's Tomb

*H*aji Begum, one of Humayun's widow, built one of the most spectacular Mughal buildings – Humayun's tomb – nine years after his death in 1565. It is the first building of Mughal architecture built in India with high arches and double dome. Humayun's tomb, in Delhi is one of the first garden tomb in the Indian subcontinent.

Sayed Muhammad Ibn Mirak Ghiyasuddin and his father Mirak Ghiyasuddin from Herat designed the tomb on the banks of the River Yamuna. The tomb design was based on Islamic paradise gardens. The complex of Humayun's tomb contains many small monuments, chief among them are black and yellow marble tomb of Haji Begum and the tomb of Humayun's barber referred as *nai ka gumbad*.

The last Mughal Emperor, Bahadur Shah Zafar, was arrested here by the British soldiers. The Aga Khan Trust took over the restoration project of the Tomb and completed it in 2003 at the cost of US $650,300. Aga Khan Trust has revived the old glory of this magnificent building and has made it really a garden of paradise by planting over 2500 trees and the plants including mango, lemon, neem, hibiscus and jasmine cuttings, long-dormant fountains have also come to life.

The tomb of Humayun, the second Mughal emperor, is an architectural wonder, and is also known as Delhi's Taj.

The Regal Purana Qila

When Humayun decided to make a city of his own he decided on the site of the ancient city of Indraprastha. Purana Qila was built in the year 1534 and the city was called Din-Panah which means 'Refuge of the Faithful'. Humayun wanted this city to be a place for scholars and learned people. Unfortunately, his Afghan chieftain, Sher Shah Suri, defeated him in the year 1540 and renamed the city as Shergarh. He built many buildings in site like Sher Mandal and a mosque called Qila-i-Kuhna Masjid, which is built skillfully in marble and red sandstone.

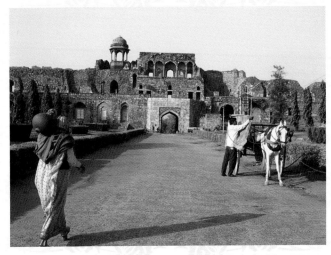

The west-side view called Bara Darwaza of Purana Qila.

The crumbling rampart of Purana Qila. The surrounding areas house the Zoological gardens and a lake where one can go boating.

In 1555, Humayun recaptured the city and lived in Purana Qila till he died. Humayun very handsomely completed the city and even used several buildings built by Sher Shah like Sher Mandal as his library and tripped to his death from its steps.

Humayun was the only Mughal emperor who built a city in Delhi and did not give it his own name. The Fort has gates on three sides and a lake on the fourth sides. In the north is Talaqi Darwaza which was built by Humayun, in the south is Humayun Darwaza built by Sher Shah, and in the west is Bara Darwaza which is used by the tourist today.

TANGERINE SHAPED LAMB KOFTAS IN RICH GRAVY
Qaliya Naranj

PREPARATION TIME: 1 HR. • COOKING TIME: 1 HR. • SERVES: 4

Ingredients

Lamb, cut into pieces	750 gm / 26 oz	Cinnamon (*dalchini*), 1″ sticks	2
Pistachios (*pista*), peeled	½ cup / 70 gm / 2¼ oz	Cloves (*laung*)	6
Almonds (*badam*), blanched,		Roasted Bengal gram (*chana*) powder	2 tbsp / 20 gm
peeled	¾ cup / 90 gm / 3oz	Egg white	2
Ghee	½ cup / 110 gm / 3¼ oz	Lemon (*nimbu*) juice	1 tbsp / 15 ml
Onions, sliced	½ cup / 85 gm / 2¾ oz	Saffron (*kesar*), dissolved in water	1 tsp
Ginger (*adrak*), chopped	2 tbsp / 15 gm	Raisins (*kishmish*)	½ cup / 70 gm / 2¼ oz
Salt to taste		Rice paste	1 tbsp / 15 gm
Coriander (*dhaniya*) seeds, crushed	1 tbsp / 6 gm	Black pepper (*kali mirch*) powder	1 tbsp / 7½ gm

Method

1. Pound the pistachios and ½ cup almonds in a mortar. Make a paste of the remaining almonds. Sauté the onions in ghee till golden. Add half the lamb, ginger, salt, coriander seeds, and 1 cup water. Cook covered on low heat till tender.

2. Separate the lamb from the liquid, strain the stock and temper it with 2 cloves. Add lamb back to the stock and keep aside. Make a fine mince of the remaining lamb.

3. Sauté the cinnamon sticks and cloves in ghee. Add lamb mince and pinch of salt; cook until done. Remove and cool. Grind to paste. Add roasted Bengal gram powder and egg white. Knead to make a hard dough. Add lemon juice and saffron mixture; mix well.

4. Make flat discs with the mince and stuff with dried fruits and raisins, fold and shape to resemble tangerines. Secure the filling with orange thread. Steam the koftas then deep-fry; remove and keep aside.

5. Bring the lamb mixture to the boil, lower heat, add almond and rice paste. Sprinkle black pepper, float the koftas and simmer for 2-3 minutes.

Humayun at the celebrations held at the time of Akbar's circumcision; Mughal,
c.1603-1604; British Library.

BAKED FLOUR BREAD FLAVOURED WITH MINT
Naan-i-Tunak

PREPARATION TIME: 10 MIN. • COOKING TIME: 10 MIN. • SERVES: 4

Ingredients

Refined flour (*maida*)	1 cup / 125 gm / 4 oz	Mint (*pudina*), chopped	1 tbsp / 4 gm
Salt	a pinch	Brown cardamom (*badi elaichi*)	6
Green coriander (*hara dhaniya*),		Cloves (*laung*)	4
chopped	1 tbsp / 4 gm	Ghee	½ cup / 110 gm / 3¼ oz

Method

1. Sift the flour with salt in a bowl.
2. Grind the green coriander, mint, brown cardamom, and cloves to a fine paste with very little water.
3. Knead the flour with ghee and spice paste into a soft dough. Cover with a wet cloth and leave aside for 10 minutes.
4. Divide the dough into 8 equal portions and shape each into a ball.
5. On a rolling board dusted with dry flour, flatten and roll each ball into a paper-thin disc. Bake on iron griddle till golden brown. Repeat till all are done.

CARROT PUDDING ENRICHED WITH DRIED FRUITS
Halvaye Zardak

PREPARATION TIME: 20 MIN. • COOKING TIME: 1 HR. • SERVES: 4

Ingredients

Carrots (*gajar*), peeled, grated	500 gm / 1.1 lb	Wholemilk fudge (*khoya*),	
Milk	4 cups / 1 lt / 32 fl oz	crushed	½ cup / 50 gm / 1¾ oz
Saffron (*kesar*)	1 tsp	Almonds (*badam*), blanched,	
Ghee	1 cup / 220 gm / 8 oz	cut into slivers	50 gm / 1¾ oz
Sugar	½ cup / 100 gm / 3¼ oz	Pistachios (*pista*), blanched,	
Green cardamom (*choti elaichi*)		cut into slivers	50 gm / 1¾ oz
powder	1 tsp / 5 gm	Raisins (*kishmish*)	50 gm / 1¾ oz
Rose water (*gulab jal*)	¼ cup / 50 ml / 1¾ fl oz	Gold leaves (*varq*)	3-4

Method

1. Cook the carrots on low heat until the moisture evaporates. Add milk and ½ tsp saffron and continue to cook on low heat, stirring occasionally, until the mixture is dry.
2. Add ghee and fry the mixture well.
3. Add sugar and stir-fry till the sugar dissolves and the mixture gets a rich colour. Add green cardamom powder and remaining saffron dissolved in milk; mix well. Remove from heat and bring to room temperature.
4. Add wholemilk fudge and rose water; mix well. Transfer into a serving dish and garnish with almonds, pistachios, and raisins. Decorate with gold leaves.

Akbar seated on a boulder under a tree, informs his courtiers that the slaughter of animals should cease; Mughal, c.1590; British Library.

Akbar
(1542-1605)

Name	Muhammad Akbar
Title	Jalal-ud-Din
Born at	Amarkot (Now in Pakistan)
Date of Birth	October 15, 1542
Date of Coronation	February 14, 1556
	Kalanaur (Punjab)
Zodiac Sign	Libra
Died on	October 27, 1605
Buried at	Sikandra

Emperor Akbar crosses the River Ganges astride elephants; Mughal, Akbarnama,
c.1598; National Museum of India.

orn in Amarkot, in Sind (now in Pakistan), in 1542, Akbar's childhood was spent in present day Afghanistan. At the age of 12, he re-entered India with his father's conquering army. From his Persian mother he inherited his princely manners, his love for literature and the arts, and a characteristically Persian delight in philosophical discussions. From his Turkish father came his fierce energy, his love for war, and his ability to command. Later he learned to absorb what was genuinely Indian.

At the time of Humayun's fatal accident, Akbar was in Punjab to fight his first independent battle under Bairam Khan. One of the few sensible things Humayun did was to put his heir under the guardianship of this wise and loyal man. The 13-year-old prince was crowned emperor on February 14, 1556, without any elaborate ceremony, at Kalanaur, a small town on River Ravi to the west of Gurdaspur in Punjab, and took the title Jalal-ud-Din Muhammad Akbar. The ruler was young and had spent his life in the shadow of the harem where Maham Anka, a former wet-nurse exercised a powerful influence on him in the interest of her son, Adham Khan. The day-to-day administration was in the hands of Bairam Khan, who had long served the Mughal cause with devotion.

Bairam Khan could not expect immediate loyalty from the Amirs. Under his advise Akbar first consolidated his position in Punjab and then proceeded towards Delhi. After the Battle of Panipat, Akbar occupied Delhi and Agra by 1564, and firmly seated himself on the throne of Delhi. His reign began on a low key, but after riding four years on the shoulder of Bairam Khan, Akbar at 18 was impatient to stand on his own feet. Akbar did not take long to realize that the administrative policies of his ancestors need unity and cohesion. He evolved a totally new system based on the goodwill of his subjects.

After strengthening his position in the north, Akbar diverted his attention to Rajputana. His dual policy towards the Rajputs paid him rich dividends. He had high rewards for those who submitted and relentless pressure on those who opposed. Soon the whole Rajasthan was under his control. He also entered into matrimonial alliances with the Rajas and married a Rajput princess. The first great event in putting this policy into practice was Akbar's marriage with the Princess of Amber dynasty, Jodha Bai, who was to become the mother of the next emperor, Jahangir. The initiative for such alliances came from the Rajas themselves as they had much gain from their links with the royal family.

Success came to Akbar easily and never once in his long reign did he ever suffer any humiliation of defeat in the battlefield. Over a period of 30 years, he built his kingdom into one of the most powerful empire on earth. His genius as a ruler held together a Hindustan of many diverse people, faith, and cultures. He also handed down an authority in government, which was scarcely challenged during the long reign of his three successors. He united both spiritual and secular leadership so effectively that his word was both divine and had human ordinance.

As an emperor he was always in the public eyes, therefore, he kept concealed within himself a good part of what he thought and felt. This hidden interior space gave him his character and resonance and also its mystery. Almost continuous warfare throughout the reign did not, however, prevent Akbar from devoting much of his time and energy to consolidating what he had already won and established a durable administrative system based on the foundation laid in the time of Sher Shah.

Akbar was a great patron of art and culture. His was a systematic and deliberate policy of promoting literature, architecture, painting, music, dancing, calligraphy, poetry, and other fine arts which made considerable progress under his patronage. In all these fields, he encouraged true worth without any invidious distinction. The widespread diffusion of education, the maintenance of religious freedom, restoration of law and order, introduction of various social reforms and the establishment of peace and prosperity throughout the length and breadth of the Mughal empire by introducing wise innovations are the index of a genius unsurpassed in the annals of the world. The most renowned artists and scholars adorned his court.

A sample of calligraphy as promoted by Akbar.

Nine jewels of his court, known as *Nau Ratans*, are remembered even now. He had an insatiable thirst for knowledge and had books read out to him regularly. He possessed a vast library and maintained an extensive translation department at the court, which could handle many languages including Greek. Many books were translated from Sanskrit and Turkish into Persian. The memoirs of Gulbadan Begum and Jauhar were written at his request, *Akbarnama* and *Ain-i-Akbari* by Abul Fazl. He was deeply interested in promoting madrasas to spread education. He loved buildings. Fatehpur Sikri is a reflex of the great mind of this man who built it. He was an avid sportsman and hunting was his best sport.

Besides all this, he was a gourmet and food lover. His attention towards his kitchen brought a revolution in the field of Indian gastronomy. His table was a pleasant mix of Turkish, Persian, and Indian flavours. Under his patronage, the kitchen became a separate but important department and cooks became respectable part of the royal living.

Akbar, according to the Jesuit Father Monsterrate, rarely drank wine, preferring *bhang*. He enforced prohibitions in his court but relaxed rules for the Europeans. Akbar did not like meat and took it only seasonally, to confirm to the spirit of the age and because he had the burden of the empire on him. He abstained from meat at first on all Fridays, subsequently on Sundays also, then on the first day of every solar month, then during the whole month of March and finally, during the month of his birth, October. He started his meal with yoghurt and rice and preferred simple food, but his table was sumptuous, as reported by the Father. It consisted of more than 40 courses served in great dishes. It is mentioned in the introduction that the cooked food was divided into three classes: first, food in which no meat was used was called *sufiyana*; second, food cooked with grain and meat; and third, meat cooked with spices.

Water was brought and stored in earthen pots to which a small quantity of water from the Ganges was added. Food was cooked in gold, silver, stone or earthen pots. The kitchen was guarded while the food was being cooked and nobody was allowed to enter. Food was tasted before dishing out. Gold and silver dishes were wrapped in a red cloth, copper and China in white. Mir Baqawal, after fixing his seal on each dish, also wrote the name of each dish upon the covering. Different kinds of pickles, chutneys, fresh ginger, lemon and green vegetables like mint, coriander wrapped in small bags sealed by Mir Baqawal made a part of the royal *khasa*.

Bread was cooked separately in *rikab-khanah* (bakery). It was of two kinds, the *buzurg tanuri*, the one baked in an oven was made big or small in size according to the need, and the *tanak tabqi*, baked on an iron plate. The latter was prepared in many ways. One type was known as chapatti, which at times was made out of *khushka*. The *khasah* chapatti contained quite a large proportion of refined flour and was brought to the table hot. In the reign of Shah Jahan, three more varieties were added: *khajura*, it was white in colour and good in quality, *roghni*, fine and delicate made with flour and ghee, and *mithi roghni* which contained sugar.

The *Ain-i-Akbari* mentions a dish in Akbar's royal kitchen which is exactly like the present day *kulfi* (a frozen dessert made of a mixture of reduced milk, pistachios, and saffron, and sealed with dough in a conical metal device).

His alliance with the Rajputs, brought a traditional Rajasthani flavour to the royal table. The deserts of Rajasthan provided good hunt to the Rajput hunters and the emperor's favourite sport was hunting. Many dishes were also developed and cooked on the hunting ground in the underground pits. Even today this style of cooking is prevalent in Rajasthan (only rabbit has been replaced by chicken). Akbar mostly dined privately and ate only once in 24 hours. Only on festive days he ate with his courtiers. Before eating he set apart food for the poor and then started his meal with milk or yoghurt.

Akbar's sons were a great source of anxiety to him. However, on his last few days he nominated Salim as his successor. In Agra, Akbar became ill with severe diarrhea and on October 27, 1605, Akbar, 63, breathed his last. He was buried at Sikandra in the tomb, which he had begun to build during his lifetime and was later completed by his son.

Chiteri or the lady painter painting a portrait; Mughal, 1630; National Museum of India. This rare depiction of a lady painter at work in the ladies' quarter confirms the involvement of women in the art of painting.

Akbar was undoubtedly a great emperor. He inherited India divided and ruled by different Amirs and rulers, but left it united in the form of a solid and compact empire to his successors. Akbar laid the foundation of Mughal rule in India so firmly that for a further century after his death the frontier of the empire continued to expand.

A royal feast for the Uzbeks; Mughal, 18th century;
National Museum of India.

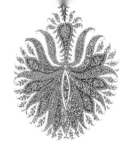

VEGETABLE PULAO

Aash Rajgir

PREPARATION TIME: 45 MIN. • COOKING TIME: 30 MIN. • SERVES: 4

Ingredients

Carrots (*gajar*), peeled, cut into pieces	4	Cloves (*laung*)	6-8
Turnips (*shalgam*), peeled, cut into pieces	3	Rice, soaked for 20 minutes,	
Spinach (*palak*), small bunch, chopped	I	drained	I½ cups / 300 gm / II oz
Ghee	¼ cup / 55 gm / I¾ oz	Saffron (*kesar*), dissolved	¼ tsp
Onions, sliced	3	Pistachios (*pista*), pounded for garnishing	
Bengal gram (*chana dal*) or Green gram (*moong dal*),		Beetroot (*chukander*), boiled, grated	½ cup
washed, drained	I¼ cups / 250 gm / 9 oz	**Ground to powder:**	
Coriander (*dhaniya*) seeds, crushed	2 tbsp / 12 gm	Cinnamon (*dalchini*), ½" stick	I
Ginger (*adrak*), chopped	I tbsp / 7½ gm	Brown cardamom (*badi elaichi*)	I
Salt to taste		Black peppercorns (*sabut kali mirch*)	I tsp / 4 gm

Method

1. Heat the ghee in a pan; sauté the onions. Add the gram and stir. Add crushed coriander seeds, ginger, salt, and 3 cups water. Cook on low heat until the gram is soft.

2. Add the vegetables except the spinach, and cook till the vegetables are soft and tender. Remove from heat and strain the liquid. Temper the liquid with cloves. Keep aside.

3. Parboil the rice in the reserved liquid and drain. Place half the rice in a pot, arrange the vegetables, spinach and cover with the remaining rice. Pour hot ghee over the rice. Add the saffron mixture and ground spice powder; cook on *dum* (see p. 20) for 10-12 minutes.

4. Serve garnished with pistachios and beetroot.

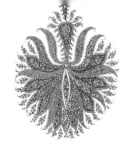

BROKEN WHEAT AND LAMB PORRIDGE
Haleem Khasa

PREPARATION TIME: 1 HR. 30 MIN. • COOKING TIME: 2 HRS. • SERVES: 4

Ingredients

Lamb, boneless, cut into medium-sized pieces	250 gm / 9 oz
Broken wheat (*dalia*), soaked overnight, drained	1 cup / 200 gm / 7 oz
Bengal gram (*chana dal*), washed, drained	¼ cup / 50 gm / 1¾ oz
Ghee	1½ cups / 330 gm / 12 oz
Onions, finely sliced	2
Cloves (*laung*)	4
Brown cardamom (*badi elaichi*)	3
Bay leaves (*tej patta*)	4
Cinnamon (*dalchini*), 1″ sticks	4
Ginger (*adrak*) paste	2 tsp / 12 gm
Garlic (*lasan*) paste	2 tsp / 12 gm
Coriander (*dhaniya*) powder	2 tsp / 10 gm
Cumin (*jeera*) powder	½ tsp / 2½ gm

Salt to taste	
Yoghurt (*dahi*), hung, whisked	1 cup / 260 gm / 9½ oz
Cudapa almonds	¼ cup
Almonds (*badam*), blanched	¼ cup / 30 gm / 1 oz
Poppy seeds (*khus khus*), soaked in water, drained	2 tbsp / 18 gm
Basmati rice, soaked for 10 minutes	2 tbsp
Milk	1 cup / 250 ml / 8 fl oz
Saffron (*kesar*), dissolved in warm milk	1 tsp
Lemon (*nimbu*) juice	1
Garam masala	1 tsp / 5 gm
For the garnishing:	
Mint (*pudina*), chopped	
Ginger, juliennes	
Black peppercorns (*sabut kali mirch*)	1 tsp / 4 gm

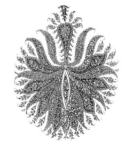

Method

1. Heat 1 cup ghee and fry the onions till brown. Remove half and keep aside for garnishing.
2. Add cloves, brown cardamom, bay leaves, and 2 cinnamon sticks; sauté for a minute. Add ginger and garlic pastes; fry for a minute. Mix coriander powder, cumin powder, salt, and $1/2$ cup water; stir well.
3. Add lamb and sauté till brown. Add yoghurt and cook until the moisture evaporates. Add broken wheat and Bengal gram to the lamb mixture, along with 6 cups water and cook on low heat until the lamb and wheat are cooked and tender. Add more water, if required, to cook the lamb if not cooked.
4. When the wheat and lamb turn soft, mash together to a porridge-like consistency. Add salt and a little water if the mixture appears too dry. Simmer for 5 minutes.
5. Grind both the almonds and poppy seeds to a fine paste.
6. Boil the rice in milk on low heat until soft and cooked. Pass through a grinder to make a paste. Keep aside.
7. Heat the remaining ghee in a pan; fry the poppy seed and almond paste. Add to lamb mixture and blend well. Mix in the saffron.
8. Gradually add the rice paste to the pan and mix well to blend.
9. Heat 2 tbsp ghee and pour over lamb mixture. Add lemon juice and sprinkle freshly ground garam masala.
10. Transfer into a bowl and serve garnished with mint, ginger, fried onions, and black peppercorns.

LENTIL COOKED WITH YOGHURT
Khasa Tilaai (Paheet)

PREPARATION TIME: 20 MIN. • COOKING TIME: 40 MIN. • SERVES: 4

Ingredients

Split and skinned		Cinnamon (*dalchini*), ½" stick	I
lentil (*arhar dal*)	2½ cups / 500 gm / 1.1 lb	Ghee	4 tbsp / 60 gm / 2 oz
Salt	I tsp	Onions, sliced	2
Yoghurt (*dahi*), hung	¼ cup / 65 gm / 2 oz	Lemon (*nimbu*) juice	I tbsp / 15 ml
Ginger (*adrak*) juice	2 tsp / 10 ml	Saffron (*kesar*), dissolved	
Cloves (*laung*)	4	in milk	¼ tsp
Green cardamom (*choti elaichi*) seeds	I tsp	Gold leaf (*varq*) for decoration	

Method

1. Boil the lentil with salt and drain.
2. Add yoghurt and ginger juice and leave aside for an hour.
3. Grind the cloves, green cardamom, and cinnamon to a fine powder. Sieve and keep aside.
4. Heat the ghee in a pan; fry the onions till golden brown. Remove one-third of the onion to be used later. Add the powdered spices and stir-fry. Add lentil mixed with yoghurt and cook on low heat adding a cup of water.
5. When the lentil is soft and cooked, add lemon juice, saffron mixture, and the reserved brown onions crushed with hand. Cover and cook on *dum* (see p. 20).
6. Serve decorated with gold leaf.

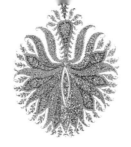

WHOLEWHEAT MILK BREAD
Roghni Roti Shahi

PREPARATION TIME: 20 MIN. • COOKING TIME: 10 MIN. • SERVES:4

Ingredients

Milk	1 cup / 250 ml / 8 fl oz	Ghee	¼ cup / 55 gm / 1¾ oz
Wholewheat flour (*atta*)	1 cup / 200 gm / 7 oz	Saffron (*kesar*)	¼ tsp
Salt to taste		Green cardamom (*choti elaichi*) powder	1 tsp / 5 gm

Method

1. Boil the milk until reduced to half.
2. Sieve the flour with salt. Add ghee, saffron, green cardamom powder, and milk. Knead to make a dough.
3. Divide the dough into 4 equal portions and roll each portion out into a disc with ½" thickness. Cook on an iron griddle (*tawa*) on low heat. Pierce the disc with a knife in the centre and around and cook pressing with a cloth on all sides. Remove when both sides have brown spots.
4. Repeat with the other portions.

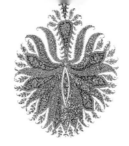

CHICKEN WRAPPED IN BREAD AND BAKED
Murgh Zameen Doz

PREPARATION TIME: 2 HRS. 30 MIN. • COOKING TIME: 1 HR. • SERVES: 4

Ingredients

Chicken, medium-sized	I	Cloves (*laung*)	3
Roomali roti	2	Mace (*javitri*)	2 blades
For the first marinade:		**For the third marinade:**	
Lemon (*nimbu*) juice	½ tsp	Yoghurt (*dahi*), hung	I cup / 260 gm / 9¼ oz
Salt to taste		Ghee	¼ cup / 55 gm / 1¾ oz
For the second marinade:		Almond (*badam*) paste	2 tbsp / 30 gm / 1 oz
Black peppercorns (*sabut kali mirch*)	8	Ginger (*adrak*) paste	I tbsp / 18 gm
Brown cardamom (*badi elaichi*)	4		
Cinnamon (*dalchini*), I″ stick	I	Chicken stock	2 cups / 600 ml / 20 fl oz
Black cumin (*shah jeera*) seeds	½ tsp / 1¼ gm	Bay leaves	2
Bay leaf (*tej patta*)	I	Saffron (*kesar*), dissolved in cream	I tsp
Nutmeg (*jaiphal*) powder	½ tsp / 2½ gm	Green coriander (*hara dhaniya*), chopped	¼ cup / 15 gm

Method

1. Clean and wash the chicken, remove the neck and the skin. Make angular and deep incisions three on each breast, two on both sides of the thighs and three on the drumsticks.

2. **For the fist marinade**, mix the ingredients in a bowl; add ½ cup water. Rub the mixture into the chicken and marinate for half an hour.

3. Grind all the ingredients of the second marinade into a thick paste. Add to the marinated chicken and leave aside for another half an hour.

4. Mix the ingredients of the third marinade and marinate chicken with it. Leave aside for 1 hour.

5. Place the chicken in a greased, wide-mouth pot (*handi*) which can fit the chicken comfortably. Add the chicken stock and bay leaves and bring to the boil. Reduce heat to low, cover and simmer for 45 minutes or until the chicken is cooked. To check insert a knife into the chicken.

6. Transfer the chicken onto a flat tray and mix in the saffron and green coriander.

7. Spread the *roomali* rotis overlapping each other on a tray. Apply ghee on the rotis and place the chicken in the middle. Wrap the chicken carefully with the roti then wrap the rotis with foil. Place the tray in the preheated oven and bake for 15 minutes at 180°C / 350°F.

Note: *A handi is an ideal cooking medium, but if not available, a charcoal grill would do just as well. The idea is to apply indirect heat on all sides of the chicken to ensure even cooking.*

Musicians performing in the Mughal court; National Museum of India.

SLOW COOKED STUFFED BITTER GOURD
Dum Ke Karele

Ingredients

Bitter gourd (*karela*), washed, skin scraped	500 gm / 1.1 lb	Cumin (*jeera*) powder	1 tsp / 5 gm
Salt	½ cup	Yoghurt (*dahi*), whisked	1 cup / 225 gm / 8 oz
Tamarind (*imli*) leaves	1 cup	Lemon (*nimbu*) juice	1 tbsp / 15 ml
Ghee	½ cup / 110 gm / 3¼ oz	Saffron (*kesar*)	2 tsp
Raisins (*kishmish*)	½ cup / 70 gm / 2¼ oz	**Ground to powder:**	
Almonds (*badam*), blanched	2 tbsp	Brown cardamom (*badi elaichi*)	2
Onions, fried	¼ cup	Black peppercorns (*sabut kali mirch*)	½ tsp / 2 gm
Onions, sliced	3 cups / 500 gm / 1.1 lb	Black cumin (*shah jeera*) seeds	½ tsp
Ginger (*adrak*), chopped	1 tbsp / 7½ gm	Cinnamon (*dalchini*), 1″ stick	1
Coriander (*dhaniya*) seeds, crushed	1 tbsp / 6 gm	Cloves (*laung*)	3

Method

1. Slit the bitter gourd lengthwise, remove the seeds, and rub salt to remove bitterness.
2. Boil the gourds with tamarind leaves. When soft remove from heat. Keep aside to cool.
3. Heat 1 tbsp ghee in a pan; fry the raisins. Add the almonds and fried onions; mix well. Remove from heat and let it cool. Fill each gourd with this mixture, and secure with a twine to seal the filling inside.
4. Heat the remaining ghee in a pan; fry onions till light golden brown. Add ginger, crushed coriander seeds and cumin powder; fry for a minute. Add yoghurt and mix well. Arrange the gourds in the pan and add the remaining filling mixture. Cover and seal the pan and cook on *dum* (see p. 20) for 10 minutes.
5. Uncover the pan, add lemon juice, saffron, and freshly ground spice powder.

Emperor Akbar inspecting the construction of Fatehpur Sikri; Mughal,
Akbarnama: *National Museum of India.*

SWEETENED RICE ENRICHED WITH DRIED FRUITS
Zard Biranj

PREPARATION TIME: 20 MIN. • COOKING TIME: 20 MIN. • SERVES: 4

Ingredients

Basmati rice	1¼ cups / 250 gm / 9 oz	Green cardamom (*choti elaichi*)	5
Rose water (*gulab jal*)	2 cups	Saffron (*kesar*), dissolved in milk	¼ tsp
Ghee	½ cup / 110 gm / 3¼ oz	Sugar	1¼ cups / 250 gm / 9 oz
Almonds (*badam*), blanched,		Juice of lemon (*nimbu*)	½
finely sliced	2 tbsp	Pistachio (*pista*) slivers	1 tbsp
Raisins (*kishmish*), soaked in water	1 tbsp	Silver leaves (*varq*)	2
Cinnamon (*dalchini*), 1″ stick	1	Cream	1 tbsp / 15 ml

Method

1. Wash and soak the rice in rose water for 10 minutes. Drain.
2. Heat the ghee in a pan; fry the almonds and raisins lightly. Remove and keep aside.
3. Reheat the ghee, fry cinnamon stick and green cardamom till the cardamom starts spluttering. Remove from heat.
4. Add rice and double the amount of water. (If rice is 1 cup add 2 cups of water). Add saffron and cook on medium heat till the rice is two third done.
5. Add fried almonds and raisins, sugar, and lemon juice; cook covered on *dum* (see p. 20).
6. Serve decorated with pistachio slivers, silver leaves and a dot of cream on top.

Jahangir enjoying wine and song; Mughal, 17th century; National Museum of India.

Jahangir
(1569-1627)

NAME	MUHAMMAD JAHANGIR (SALIM)
TITLE	NUR-UD-DIN
BORN AT	FATEHPUR SIKRI (AGRA)
DATE OF BIRTH	AUGUST 31, 1569
DATE OF CORONATION	NOVEMBER 3, 1605
ZODIAC SIGN	LEO
DIED ON	OCTOBER 28, 1627
BURIED AT	LAHORE

Jahangir with the imperial orb appearing at a jharokha *(viewing window for official appearances) and Jesus with the cross; Mughal, c.1618–20; National Museum of India.*

A week after the death of Akbar, November 3, 1605, shortly after sunrise, 36-year-old Salim ascended the imperial throne in Agra and took the title Nur-ud-Din Muhammad Jahangir. He was an intelligent and an able young man, well educated with broad cultural interest. Very little is known about his childhood. He was born on August 31, 1659, in the hermitage of Sheikh Salim Chishti. Akbar doted on him and called him Shaikhu Baba; it is unfortunate that the relationship between father and son got bitter later, due to Salim's infatuation towards Anarkali and Mehr-un-Nisa.

At the age of seven, he was given nominal charge of the Mewar campaign and at the age of 12 he accompanied his father on the Kabul campaign. To initiate him into the administrative process, under the guardianship of Abdur-Rahim Khan-i-Khanan, he was given charge of two departments, justice and celebration. Ruling over a vast empire, which was prosperous and peaceful, Jahangir enjoyed riches beyond imagination. He did take his ceremonial duties seriously, but his passion remained hunting, drinking, and jewel connoisseurship. His life was not filled with adventures or excitement; he never fought a battle himself but did remain close by to watch the action.

Despite his Rajput mother, Jahangir seems to have disliked the Indian plains. He preferred Lahore to Delhi or Agra, but it was Kashmir which he loved best and it was during his reign that regular journeys across Pir Panjal became an established feature of court life. It was in Kashmir, where he could escape the ceaseless rounds of business and public appearances which enveloped him in the cities of the plains and enter an idyllic private world where he could indulge in his love of nature and feminine company, undisturbed.

Despite an acute intelligence, Jahangir was indifferent to the larger interest of the empire. He lacked any obvious inclination for warfare and was bored by the humdrum details of day-to-day administration. Self-indulgent and sensual, a compulsive drinker, he left the reigns of the empire in the hands of his beloved wife, Nur Jahan.

Jahangir's ambition was to be remembered as a just emperor. He set up a chain of justice to give access to the oppressed to reach out to the king and demand justice. He also promulgated a set of 12 ordinances to improve the administration of his kingdom. Jahangir is the most endearing of the Mughals who dared to show the human face behind the pharaonic persona of the emperor.

The most romantic event of Jahangir's reign was his marriage to Mehr-un-Nisa, the most beautiful daughter of Mirza Ghiyas Baig, a native of Tehran. She was given the title of Nur Jahan by the emperor. She was the most beloved wife of the emperor and as a token of his love for her, Jahangir put her name on coinage along with his own. Although Nur Jahan came late in Jahangir's life, but she gradually seized the reigns of power from him and made herself supreme authority. As Jahangir mentions, 'The 11 years from his marriage to Nur Jahan in 1611 to the outbreak of rebellion by Shah Jahan in1622 were the best years of his life. They were years of peace and prosperity.'

During the reign of Jahangir, India was visited by a number of foreigners, the Portuguese, the Dutch, and the English, all wanting to establish friendly relations with the Mughal emperor. Finally in 1615, Sir Thomas Roe, a representative of the King of

A royal seal.

England, succeeded in getting a *firman* from the emperor to build a factory in Surat. Many European travellers who visited India then have left their impressions about the court and the country. Jahangir himself wrote his autobiography called *Tuzak-i-Jahangiri* with the help of two historians, Muhammad Hadi and Mutamid Khan. Under Jahangir, the imperial court was the cradle of the sage and the scholars, the poets and the painters. Great as was Jahangir's love for learning, no less was his zeal for the extension of education in his kingdom. He gave fresh impetus to the school of his father's creation. His patronage raised the Indian painter's art to the highest pitch, they copied the finest European paintings to perfection, and on one occasion even Roe could not differentiate between them.

Jahangir surpassed his father in aesthetic tastes. He developed a large number of gardens in his kingdom of which Shalimar Garden and Nishat Garden, in Kashmir, keep his memory alive even today. He was alive to nature and his memoirs are rich with graphic details of the places he visited. In Kabul, he got a round basin carved and filled with wine, he held great feasts there. Like his father, Jahangir had special fondness for Lahore and the surrounding regions. He lavishly adorned the city of Lahore with mosques, palaces, and gardens. In reality, he made Lahore a city of gardens. During his reign, the Punjab enjoyed an extended period of peace and prosperity.

Jahangir was fastidious regarding food. While hunting, he often cut open animals of hunt to make sure their flesh was not disagreeable to him. Like his father, he also ate vegetarian food on Sundays and Thursdays. No animal was slaughtered on these days. On abstinence days, he took *lazizah*, a kind of *khichdi*, to which he had taken a liking during his stay in Gujarat. This dish was prepared in the Gujarati style with millet, pulses, and rice. He said, 'It had a good flavour and agreed with him.'

As he spent most of his time between Punjab and Kashmir, his table got richer with flavours of these two places. A large number of cooks and artisans had come from Samarqand to Kashmir with Timur and did not return. These cooks were experts and produced mouth-watering banquets for the emperor. The food was cooked overnight on low heat and a meal fit for the king was produced. Today, the present generation of these cooks call themselves Wazas, and prepare the spread under the name, Wazwaan for special occasions.

Jahangir appreciated good food and enjoyed eating. He was a fine judge of different kinds of flesh. He preferred that of black partridge, the large quail, of fat kid, and of rohu. He also loved a preparation called *dopiyazah* of neelgai. He was very fond of fish but with scales. Once when he was in Gujarat, he had not eaten fish for 11 months, and when he was presented with rohu he rewarded the man with a horse. He enjoyed drinking camel milk. Like his father, he also ate and drank in the company of yogis on Shivratri.

Like Akbar, he loved fruits especially mangoes. He even exempted the cultivation of fruits from tax and encouraged horticulture. In Kashmir, he picked cherries himself from his private garden. The great Mughal only drank the Ganges water. Jahangir carried

The bullock cart; a painting by Abul Hasan. This unmistakably Persian subject was painted for Jahangir; Mughal, c.1604; National Museum of India.

his water whenever he went. His drinking water was carried on a golden tray which contained a salver and cups, they bore covering and the whole of it was placed in a cotton bag, thus no water or dust could get into it. He loved wine when still a prince, later it affected his health and was advised not to drink heavily.

On October 28, 1627, Jahangir died at the age of 58 after ruling the vast empire for 22 years. He was buried in Lahore, the city of his gardens.

LAMB KEBABS
Yakhni Kebab

PREPARATION TIME: 1 HR. • COOKING TIME: 20 MIN. • SERVES: 4

Ingredients

Lamb with bones, cleaned	750 gm / 26 oz	Cinnamon (*dalchini*), 1″ stick	1
Onion, sliced	1	Black cumin (*shah jeera*) seeds	¼ tsp
Ginger (*adrak*), chopped	1 tbsp / 7½ gm	Black pepper (*kali mirch*) powder	1 tsp / 5 gm
Salt to taste		Salt	¼ tsp
Ghee	1 cup / 220 gm / 8 oz	Poppy seeds (*khus khus*), soaked for 1 hour,	
Cloves (*laung*)	6	drained, ground to paste	1 tbsp / 9 gm
Bengal gram (*chana dal*)	½ cup / 100 gm / 3¼ oz	Saffron (*kesar*)	½ tsp
Browned onion	2 tbsp	Green coriander (*hara dhaniya*), chopped	1 tbsp / 4 gm
Yoghurt (*dahi*)	1 tbsp / 15 gm	Roasted Bengal gram powder	1 tbsp / 9 gm
Brown cardamom (*badi elaichi*)	2	Ghee for shallow-frying	

Method

1. Cook the lamb with onion, ginger, salt, and 4 cups water to make *yakhni* on medium heat; bring to the boil. Reduce heat, cover and simmer until the lamb is tender (add more water, if required). Remove the lamb from the stock and cool, separate meat from the bones, strain the stock and reserve.

2. Temper the stock five times with cloves in very hot ghee. Add Bengal gram and bring to the boil. Cook on low heat until the gram is soft and has absorbed the stock. Remove from heat and cool.

3. Make a fine paste of browned onion and yoghurt; keep aside.

4. Add shredded meat, whole spices, black pepper powder and salt to cooked Bengal gram. Grind to make a smooth paste. Add browned onion paste and the remaining ingredients except ghee. Cook the mixture for a minute till it becomes dry. Remove and cool. Check seasoning.

5. Divide the mixture into 16 equal portions, flatten each portion into a patty and shallow-fry in ghee until golden and crisp on both side. Serve with lemon wedges.

Jahangir dispensing food at Ajmer; Jahangirnama, Mughal, c.1620;
National Museum of India.

FISH PATTIES
Kebab-e-Mahi

PREPARATION TIME: 1 HR. • COOKING TIME: 15 MIN. • SERVES: 4

Ingredients

Fish, rohu, cut into pieces	750 gm / 26 oz	Fennel (*moti saunf*) seeds	1 tbsp / 7½ gm
Gram flour (*besan*)	½ cup / 75 gm / 2½ oz	Cumin (*jeera*) seeds	1 tbsp / 9 gm
Mustard oil	2 tbsp / 30 ml / 1 fl oz	Lamb mince	¼ cup
Turmeric (*haldi*) powder	1 tsp / 5 gm	Gram flour, roasted	2 tbsp / 15 gm
Salt to taste		Onion, grated	1 tbsp
Yoghurt (*dahi*), whisked	½ cup / 110 gm / 3¼ oz	Ginger (*adrak*), grated	1 tsp / 6 gm
Lemon (*nimbu*) leaves	a few	Yellow lentil (*moong pithi*), soaked,	
Lemon juice	2 tbsp / 30 ml / 1 fl oz	ground	2 tbsp
Bay leaves (*tej patta*)	1	Poppy (*khus khus*) seed paste	1 tbsp / 15 gm
Ghee	¼ cup / 55 gm / 1¾ oz	White of eggs	4
Onion, medium-sized, sliced	1	Sour yoghurt	½ tbsp
Cinnamon (*dalchini*), 2" sticks	2	Salt to taste	
Cloves (*laung*)	8	Ghee for frying	
Brown cardamom (*badi elaichi*)	4	Gold leaves (*varq*)	10
Black peppercorns (*sabut kali mirch*)	1 tsp / 4 gm	Silver leaves	10
Coriander (*dhaniya*) seeds	1 tbsp / 6 gm		

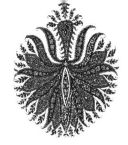

Method

1. Rub gram flour all over the fish and keep aside for 5 minutes. Wash with cold water.
2. Mix mustard oil with turmeric powder and salt; rub this mixture evenly over the fish and keep aside for an hour.
3. Again wash the fish with cold water and marinate in whisked yoghurt for 15 minutes. Remove and rub gram flour over the fish. Wash with cold water.
4. Boil the fish with fresh lemon leaves; remove and drain. Now the fish is ready to be cooked.
5. Boil the fish with lemon juice, salt, and bay leaves on low heat until tender. Remove the pan from the heat and separate the fish. Keep aside to cool. Remove the bones and mash to a smooth paste.
6. Heat the ghee in a pan; add half the onion and sauté until brown. Add half of the whole spices and stir. Add the lamb mince and cook on medium heat until mince is nicely fried and dry.
7. Make a powder of the reserved whole spices.
8. Mix the gram flour and cooked lamb mince with grated onion and ginger. Grind the mixture to a silky paste.
9. Add yellow lentil and poppy seed pastes together with egg white, sour yoghurt, freshly ground whole spices, and salt to lamb mince paste. Add fish paste; mix well and smoke (see p. 20 *dhungar*) the mixture. Divide the mixture into 8 equal parts and shape them into patties.
10. Heat the ghee in a pan; fry the patties until crisp and brown. Remove and cover each patty alternately in silver and gold leaves.
11. Serve hot with lemon slices on the side.

Arts and Jewels of Jahangir

Above: *The clasp of a Mughal bracelet (front and back) with beautiful floral and bird motifs, is executed using the champleve technique.*
Below: *Exquisitely damascend Mughal sword hilts.*

Jahangir's love for art, gems and jewels was no less than his father. He set up his independent studio in Allahabad, even before he ascended the throne under the Persian painters Aqa Raza and his son, Abu Hasan. After he assumed the power, he encouraged artists to develop their own individual style, traits and talents, and each to have specialized area. Pleasures and pastimes of court life, portraits, study of birds, animals, and flowers, scenes derived from reproduces of European art, studies of holy men were some of Jahangir's favourite subjects.

Many of the paintings produced at the imperial court are preserved in the album, assembled for Jahangir and his son, Shah Jahan. The Muraqqah-e-Gulshan is the most spectacular. Many of the finest paintings by Jahangir's master painters have magnificent borders decorated with a wide variety of floral and geometrical designs. These paintings give a clear indication of Jahangir as a patron, collector, and connoisseur of the arts, revealing a person with a wide range of taste and a curious mind. Jahangir esteemed the art of painting and honored his painters. Abu Hasan was designated Nadir-uz-Zaman (Wonder of the Ages) and Ustad Mansur was given the title of Nadir-ul-Asr (Wonder of the Time). Bishn Das, Manohar, Govardhan, and Daulat are other important painters of his reign.

Jahangir had great fondness for jewellery as well. He commissioned artists and jewellers from all over the empire and from abroad to design and make some of the most exquisite items for his personal adornment and for his beloved queen. These jewellers combined the Persian techniques with Indian motifs to produce some of the finest pieces of enamelled jewellery. These pieces are a perfect reflection of the rich composite culture of the subcontinent during Mughal rule, it is unfortunate that very few examples of Mughal jewellery and enamel work of the period have survived in the world museums. The urge to hold and touch some of these glittering objects locked behind glass cases is persistent,

Kundan jewellery is probably the oldest form of jewel crafting in India. It is said that *kundan* work was brought to Rajasthan from Delhi during the Mughal period. Most of the pieces made for the emperor were decorated with red poppy flower and green foliage on white background.

The world's greatest collection of large, red spinels is that of the crown jewels of Iran. A companion piece of 270 carat has emperor Jahangir's name engraved upon it, and a gold box whose entire surface is covered with 93 carved emeralds.

Hiuen-Tsang's travel accounts also mention the use of jade in India. An English Sea Captain, Hawkins, who visited Jahangir's court in 1613 found 500 cups made of rubies, emeralds, jade, and other semi-precious and precious stones. Fashioning jade to exquisite art forms is a highly skilled but difficult and slow process. Finished jade objects were often damascened with gold or silver or else enamelled or studded with jewels, not only for their external beauty but also to grant them the royal status. Other notable examples of decorative jade piecesof art of Jahangir's period are spectacular *huqqas*, studded plates, betel and spice-boxes, cups, bowls, plaques, tumblers, etc.

Top: *This gem-studded enamelled gold head ornament (jhumar) hung with enamelled fish dangling from pearls, has a dancing peacock crafted in enamel.*
Left: *The beautiful enamelled boxes is a blend of Persian techniques with Indian motifs.*

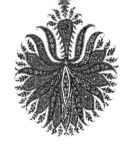

LAMB ESCALLOPS
Pasande Noor Mahli

Ingredients

Lamb, boneless, cut into cubes	750 gm / 26 oz	Rose petals (*gulab pankhuri*), dried	¼ cup
Black peppercorns (*sabut kali mirch*)	I tsp / 4 gm	Poppy seeds (*khus khus*), roasted,	
Black cumin (*shah jeera*) seeds	I tsp / 2½ gm	ground to paste	2 tsp / 6 gm
Brown cardamom (*badi elaichi*)	4	Almonds (*badam*), blanched,	
Cloves (*laung*)	5	ground to paste	I½ tbsp
Cinnamon (*dalchini*), I″ stick	I	Nutmeg (*jaiphal*) powder	¼ tsp
Yoghurt (*dahi*)	I cup / 225 gm / 8 oz	Mace (*javitri*) powder	¼ tsp
Ginger (*adrak*) paste	2 tsp / 12 gm	Green cardamom (*choti elaichi*) powder	I tsp / 5 gm
Raw papaya paste	2 tsp / 10 gm	Salt to taste	
Saffron (*kesar*)	I tsp	Pistachio (*pista*) slivers	2 tbsp
Coconut (*nariyal*) powder, roasted	2 tbsp / 30 gm / I oz	Silver leaves (*varq*)	3
Red chilli powder	2 tsp / 10 gm	Rose petals, fresh	¼ cup

Method

1. Beat the lamb with the back of a knife into flat pieces, gently wash and keep aside.
2. Dry-roast the whole spices on an iron griddle (*tawa*). Remove and grind to a fine powder.
3. Whisk yoghurt with salt, ginger paste, raw papaya paste, saffron, coconut powder, red chilli powder, roasted spice powder, dried rose petals, poppy seed and almond pastes; mix well. Marinate the lamb in this mixture for 2 hours.
4. Place the marinated lamb in a pan. Cover and cook on low heat until the moisture evaporates and the lamb is soft and well cooked.
5. Sprinkle the spice powder and salt; and cook on *dum* (see p. 20) for 5-7 minutes.
6. Serve garnished with pistachios, silver leaves, and fresh rose petals.

LAMB COOKED WITH MANGOES
Qaliya Amba

PREPARATION: 1 HR. 30 MIN. • COOKING TIME: 35 MIN. • SERVES: 4

Ingredients

Lamb, cut into		Almonds (*badam*), pounded	2 tbsp
medium-sized pieces	800 gm / 28 oz	Raisins (*kishmish*)	2 tbsp
Raw mangoes (*kairi*)	600 gm / 22 oz	Sugar	¾ cup / 150 gm / 5 oz
Onions, sliced	2	Rice paste	1 tbsp / 15 gm
Ginger (*adrak*), chopped	1 tbsp / 7½ gm	Cinnamon (*dalchini*), 1″ stick	1
Coriander (*dhaniya*) seeds, crushed	1 tbsp / 6 gm	Brown cardamom (*badi elaichi*)	1
Salt to taste		Black peppercorns (*sabut kali mirch*)	1 tsp / 4 gm
Cloves (*laung*)	6	Saffron (*kesar*)	½ tsp
Pistachios (*pista*), pounded	2 tbsp	Silver leaves (*varq*)	4

Method

1. Cook the lamb with onions, ginger, crushed coriander seeds, salt, and 3 cups water. When the lamb is tender, remove from heat and strain the liquid; separate the lamb.
2. Add the lamb pieces to the stock and temper with cloves. Add the dried fruits and keep aside.
3. Prepare sugar syrup of one-string consistency.
4. Cook half of the sliced mangoes on low heat in the sugar syrup. When tender, remove and keep aside. Save the sugar syrup to be used later.
5. Boil the remaining mangoes till soft. Remove, squeeze with hands to make pulp. Strain the pulp, blend it with the reserved sugar syrup, and bring to one boil on low heat. Add to the stock and continue cooking on low heat.
6. When the gravy is consistent, add the reserved mango, rice paste, freshly ground whole spices, and saffron; simmer for 5-7 minutes.
7. Serve decorated with silver leaves.

RICE AND GREEN GRAM WITH LAMB KOFTAS

Lazeezan

PREPARATION TIME: 40 MIN. • COOKING TIME: 55 MIN. • SERVES: 4

Ingredients

Lamb, boneless, cut into pieces	250 gm / 9 oz	Cloves (*laung*)	6
Lamb knuckles	4	Ghee	¾ cup / 165 gm / 5¾ gm
Onions, sliced	¾ cup / 130 gm / 4½ oz	Silver leaves (*varq*)	2
Ginger (*adrak*), chopped	2 tbsp / 15 gm	Green gram (*moong dal*), washed	1 cup / 200 gm / 7 oz
Salt to taste		Rice	1 cup / 200 gm / 7 oz
Coriander (*dhaniya*) seeds, crushed	2 tbsp / 12 gm	Saffron (*kesar*), dissolved in milk	½ tsp
Almonds (*badam*), blanched,		Cinnamon (*dalchini*), 1″ stick	1
peeled	¼ cup / 30 gm / 1 oz	Brown cardamom (*badi elaichi*)	1
Rice paste	1 tbsp / 15 gm	Almond, cut into slivers	2 tbsp
Cream	1 cup / 240 ml / 8 fl oz	Rose petals (*gulab pankhuri*)	¼ cup

Method

1. Make *yakhni* with lamb pieces and knuckles, adding half of the onion slices, ginger, salt, and 1 tbsp coriander seeds.

2. Remove the boneless lamb when soft and tender. Continue cooking the lamb knuckles until tender and the meat has left the bones. Remove the knuckles from the stock. Separate the bones, mash the meat and mix with the stock. Strain the stock through a muslin cloth and keep aside.

3. Grind the almonds with rice paste and the remaining coriander seeds. Mix with the cream and add to the stock. Temper the stock twice with cloves.

4. Mash half the boneless lamb with hand (reserve half) and grind to a silky paste. Divide the paste equally and shape into small koftas.

5. Heat the ghee in a pan; deep-fry the koftas. Remove and keep aside. When cool, cover each kofta with silver leaves and keep aside.

6. Fry the remaining onion slices in the same ghee until golden brown.

7. Parboil the rice and green gram together with enough water until the gram is tender. Drain and keep aside.

8. Arrange the remaining pieces of boneless lamb in the bottom of a pan, cover with cooked rice and green gram mixture, then place the koftas over them, topped with fried onion, saffron mixture, and freshly ground whole spices (cinnamon, and brown cardamom). Pour the stock over the koftas, cover and cook on *dum* (see p. 20).

9. While serving, garnish with almond slivers and rose petals.

91

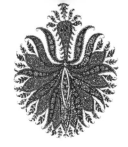

POUNDED LAMB BALLS IN YOGHURT SAUCE
Gushtaba

PREPARATION TIME: 1 HR. • COOKING TIME: 45 MIN. • SERVES: 4

Ingredients

Lamb, boneless	1½ kg / 3.3 lb	Ghee	1 tbsp / 15 gm
Salt to taste		Cinnamon (*dalchini*), 1″ sticks	2
Dried ginger (*sonth*)	3 tsp / 15 gm	Yoghurt (*dahi*), whisked	1 kg / 2.2 lb
Brown cardamom (*badi elaichi*),		Fennel (*moti saunf*) powder	2 tsp / 10 gm
powdered	1 tsp / 5 gm	Salt to taste	

Method

1. On a smooth-surfaced stone, pound the lamb with a wooden mallet till it turns to pulp. Add salt, 1 tsp dried ginger, and brown cardamom powder, continue to pound.
2. Divide the pulp into equal portions and shape into round balls, 2″ in diameter. Boil the balls in adequate quantity of water in a pan. Stir them gently for about 5 minutes, be careful not to break the meat balls. Remove and keep aside.
3. Heat the ghee in a pan; add cinnamon sticks, and yoghurt; stir till it changes colour and turns light brown. Add 3 cups water and the remaining dried ginger, fennel powder, and the lamb balls. Boil for 5 minutes, then simmer for about 15 minutes. Check seasoning and remove from heat.
4. Serve hot in individual bowls.

SWEETENED WHEAT BALLS WITH DRIED FRUITS
Maleedah Gujarati

PREPARATION TIME: 30 MIN. • COOKING TIME: 20 MIN. • SERVES: 4

Ingredients

Wholewheat flour		Pine nuts (*chilgoza*), pounded	2 tbsp
(*atta*)	2½ cups / 500 gm / 1.1 lb	Raisins (*kishmish*)	2 tbsp
Ghee	1¼ cups / 275 gm / 10 oz	Sugar candy (*mishri*), crushed	¼ cup
Sugar	¾ cup / 150 gm / 5 oz	Coconut (*nariyal*), roasted	2 tbsp
Almonds (*badam*), pounded	2 tbsp	Green cardamom (*choti elaichi*) seeds	2 tbsp
Pistachios (*pista*), pounded	2 tbsp	Cinnamon (*dalchini*) powder	1 tbsp / 7½ gm

Method

1. Sift the wholewheat flour in a bowl. Add 1 cup ghee and knead to form a semi-hard dough. Divide the dough equally into small portions.

2. Roll each portion out into a small disc and bake on iron griddle (*tawa*) till brown. Remove and break into small pieces while still warm, using both hands or pound in a mortar.

3. In a bowl, add sugar, remaining ghee, pounded dried fruits, sugar candy, broken pieces of roti, and the remaining ingredients. Mix well with silver leaf.

4. Divide the mixture equally into small portions and shape into balls. Remove and serve on a bed of rose petals.

Shah Jahan in durbar holding a ruby in his left hand. On the left is Aurangzeb who salutes his father; Mughal, c.1650; British Library.

Shah Jahan

1592-1666

NAME	GHIYAS-UD-DIN MUHAMMAD
TITLE	SHAH JAHAN (KHURRAM)
BORN AT	LAHORE
DATE OF BIRTH	JANUARY 5, 1592
DATE OF CORONATION	NOVEMBER 16, 1627
ZODIAC SIGN	CAPRICORN
DIED ON	JANUARY 22, 1666
BURIED AT	AGRA (TAJ MAHAL)

hah Jahan was born on the night of January 5, 1592, in Lahore, to a Rajput princess Jagat Gosain, daughter of Raja Udai Singh Rathore. Akbar named him Khurram. In the summer of 1607, when Khurram was 16 he was engaged to Asaf Khan's daughter, Arjumand Banu Begun, and was appointed commander of 8000 cavalry, shortly after, he was formally designated heir apparent and the seal of the empire was given to him. His engagement to Arjumand Banu lasted for 4 years. In 1612, when he was 20 and she 19, a royal wedding took place. She was the most beloved wife of the emperor. He loved her quite as much for her physical attraction as for her intellectual attainments. She bore him 14 children and remained a constant source of strength to him till she passed away, in 1631 at Burhanpur, in child labour. Shah Jahan was totally devastated after her death; the emperor in the white marble mausoleum monument of love and fidelity has safely preserved her memory.

Khurram remained favourite of Jahangir till 1622 and then unexpectedly turned rebel to the emperor's dismay. After the death of Jahangir, with the help of his father-in-law, Asaf Khan, Khurram was crowned on November 16, 1627, at Agra and assumed the title of Shah Jahan. Arjumand Banu was given the title of Mumtaz Mahal.

Shah Jahan was not made for the glories of the conquest; he regarded war as inhuman and was not a great general himself. His reign was essentially a period of peace, in which literature flourished, education made mighty strides, architecture, painting, poetry, and music progressed in leap and bounds. The splendour of his court and glory of his reign with all their dazzle and oriental colours are a by-word to everyone who has little acquaintance with Indian history.

During the early years of his reign, Shah Jahan seems to have preferred Agra to Delhi as place of residence and, no doubt, his preference was partly due to his preoccupation with the construction of Taj Mahal, yet notwithstanding the splendour of Agra and the scale of the building operation which he had

A seal of Shah Jahan

undertaken there. In the eleventh year of his reign, he thought of shifting his capital from Agra to Delhi. Shah Jahan resolved to found a new capital city at Delhi called Shahjahanabad. The location of this seventh city of Delhi, Shahjahanabad or Old Delhi, as it is called now, was just north of Kotla Firuz Shah and included within its limits part of the area formerly belonging to the fifth city, Firuzabad, built by Firuz Shah Tughlaq in the second half of the fourteenth century. Within a period of nine years, the famous Red Fort sprang into existence in all its glory and grandeur. Shah Jahan held a ten-day-long celebration to inaugurate Shahjahanabad. He entered the new capital on April 18, 1648, to mount the jewelled throne at the time specified by the court astrologer.

The reign of Shah Jahan is rendered memorable in history for the excellence of its architecture, Taj — a dream in marble — and the fort of Shahjahanabad.

Shah Jahan also had fine taste for gardens — the Shalimar Garden in Lahore, the gardens at Red Fort of Delhi and Taj in Agra were most voluptuous of their class in the Mughal Empire. Himself a cultured king and a refined scholar, Shah Jahan was a distinguished patron of letters. The celebrated *Padshahnamah* written by

Muhammad Amin-i-Qazwini under the direction of the emperor is a treasure house of research for the historians and gives a detailed account of his reign. To the Europeans who visited Delhi during the reign of Shah Jahan, his court represented the acme of oriental splendour, wealth, and unfettered absolutism. Few who had seen the emperor at the height of his power, seated on the peacock throne, could never have imagined that his last days would be so utterly tragic.

The closing years of the glorious reign of Shah Jahan were darkened by a war of succession. When he fell ill, the four princes were in possession of the different provinces and in the absence of a well defined law of succession each one tried to grab the power. The war could have been prevented if Shah Jahan had re-assured his authority immediately after his recovery but, unfortunately, misjudging the trends of events, he continued favouring his eldest son, Dara. This resulted in the fury of Aurangzeb who did achieve a decisive victory over others. He marched towards Agra and imprisoned his father in his palace and kept him captive for eight full years.

The Portuguese relationship with the Mughals had already been established a long time back, which was best on the control of trade routes. Hence Shah Jahan's reign saw yet another additional ingredient in the royal dishes – the chilli. Chilli was very similar to long pepper in appliance and, therefore, did not look too unfamiliar to the royal chefs. Vegetables like potatoes and tomatoes also appeared on the scene and the food of Red Fort became rich in colour, varied in variety, and hot in taste as compared to the bland food of its ancestors. *Qormas* and *qaliyas*, biryani and kebabs, vegetables in different garbs, besides European cakes and puddings adorned the table of Red Fort.

Bent in age and broken in health, the most magnificent monarch of the Mughal dynasty passed away in 1666 as a captive of his son who did not care to attend his funeral. Shah Jahan was buried in Agra, in the Taj Mahal, next to his beloved queen; even death has not been able to separate them.

Funeral procession of Shah Jahan at Agra; Mughal, 18th century; British Library.

A Prince and his favourites enjoying wine and music; Mughal, c. 1700;
National Museum of India.

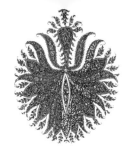

BROKEN WHEAT AND LAMB COOKED TO PERFECTION
Harisa Badshahi

PREPARATION TIME: 1 HR. 30 MIN. • COOKING TIME: 45 MIN. • SERVES: 4

Ingredients

Broken wheat (*dalia*), soaked overnight, drained	2½ cups / 500 gm / 1.1 lb
Lamb, cut into pieces	500 gm / 1.1 lb
Ginger (*adrak*), chopped	2 tbsp / 15 gm
Garlic (*lasan*), crushed	1 tbsp
Coriander (*dhaniya*) seeds, crushed	2 tbsp / 12 gm
Salt to taste	
Cumin (*jeera*) seeds	1 tsp / 3 gm
Fennel (*moti saunf*) seeds	2 tbsp / 15 gm
Rose petals (*gulab pankhuri*), dried	¼ cup
Vetiver roots (*khas ki jad*)	a small handful
Brown cardamom (*badi elaichi*)	3
Cloves (*laung*)	6
Milk	10 cups / 2½ lt
Ghee	½ cup / 110 gm / 3¼ oz
Saffron (*kesar*)	¼ tsp
Cinnamon (*dalchini*) powder	1 tsp / 5 gm
Black peppercorns (*sabut kali mirch*), crushed	1 tsp / 4 gm
Mint (*pudina*), chopped	¼ cup / 15 gm
Onions, cut into slices, fried	2

Method

1. Make *yakhni* with lamb, ginger, garlic, crushed coriander seeds, and salt in a pan.
2. Tie the next 5 ingredients in a muslin cloth and add to the pan. Cook on moderate heat until the meat is soft and tender. Discard the muslin bag. Reserve the liquid. Remove and shred the lamb into thin fibers and return to the reserved liquid. Pass the liquid through a muslin to get maximum extract. Temper the liquid with cloves (reserve one).
3. Boil the milk with broken wheat; cook on low heat, stirring constantly so that it does not stick to the bottom, till wheat is cooked. Add stock and blend well. Cook on low heat, stirring constantly, till the mixture starts thickening and begins to come off the sides of the pan. Remove from heat.
4. Heat the ghee to smoking and crack the reserved clove. Add ghee to the wheat mixture; stir well. Check seasoning. Bring mixture to one boil and simmer.
5. Before serving garnish with the remaining ingredients.

LAMB IN THICK YOGHURT SAUCE
Qaliya Talavi

PREPARATION TIME: 40 MIN. • COOKING TIME: 1 HR. 30 MIN. • SERVES: 4

Ingredients

		For the gravy:	
Lamb, boneless, flattened	300 gm / 11 oz	Bay leaf (*tej patta*)	1
Raw papaya paste	1 tbsp / 15 gm	Green cardamom (*choti elaichi*)	3
Ginger (*adrak*), grated	½ tbsp / 4 gm	Cloves	3
Mint (*pudina*), chopped	½ tbsp / 2 gm	Cinnamon (*dalchini*), 1″ stick	1
Black peppercorns (*sabut kali mirch*), crushed	1 tsp / 4 gm	Onions, sliced	2
Salt to taste		Ginger paste	½ tbsp / 9 gm
Egg white, whisked	1	Green chillies, deseeded, chopped	2
Ghee	¼ cup / 55 gm / 1¾ oz	Red chilli powder	½ tsp / 2½ gm
For the *yakhni*:		Salt to taste	
Lamb with bone	250 gm / 9 oz	Yoghurt (*dahi*)	¾ cup / 165 gm / 5½ oz
Onion, sliced	1	Poppy (*khus khus*) seed paste	¼ tbsp
Ginger (*adrak*) paste	½ tsp / 3 gm	Rice paste	¼ tbsp
Coriander (*dhaniya*), pounded	1 tbsp / 6 gm	Almond (*badam*) paste	½ tbsp
Salt to taste		Melon (*magaz*) seed paste	½ tbsp
Cloves (*laung*)	2	Green cardamom and mace powder	½ tsp
		Silver leaves (*varq*)	6

Method

1. Marinate the lamb with raw papaya paste, ginger, mint, black pepper and salt for 30 minutes.

2. **For the** *yakhni*, mix all the ingredients together, add 2 cups of water and cook till the lamb is soft. Remove from heat and separate the lamb pieces. Discard the bones and mash the meat. Add the mashed meat to the stock. Strain the stock and keep aside.

3. Heat the ghee in a pan; lift the lamb pieces from the marinade, dip in egg white and shallow-fry, on medium heat, until tender. Remove and cool.

4. Cover each piece with silver leaf and keep aside.

5. **For the gravy**, in the same oil, sauté the whole spices for a few seconds. Add the onions and fry till golden brown. Add ginger paste, green chillies, red chilli powder, salt, and ½ cup water; cook for 2 minutes.

6. Add the yoghurt and cook on low heat until oil surfaces.

7. Add all the pastes and blend well. Add the reserved stock and bring to the boil, then simmer on low heat until oil surfaces. Add green cardamom and mace powder, cover and cook on *dum* (see p. 20).

8. While serving, add lamb pieces to the gravy and garnish with almond slivers.

A Dream Fulfilled: Shah Jahan's Taj

Shah Jahan (1592-1666), the great Mughal, met Arjumand Banu when he was 15, married her when he was 20 and remained in love with her till their last days together. He rewarded her exceptional loyalty by giving her the title of Mumtaz Mahal or the Chosen One of the Palace, and the sole authority to use the Royal Seal. She encouraged him in his passion for architecture. Her demise spurred him to construct the magnificent Taj Mahal, one of the seven wonders of the world.

Shah Jahan chose the finest material for the embellishment of the monument. White marble was brought from Makrana, in Rajasthan; precious stones like crystal came from Tibet; agate from Yemen; coral from the Red Sea; onyx from Persia; and chrysolite from Europe. The marble screen enclosing the cenotaphs features an astonishing range of inlay work, some of it inset in single blocks of marble.

The cenotaphs of Mumtaz Mahal and Shah Jahan in the upper chamber of the Taj are encircled by a marble screen. All the sides of the monument except the south entrance are also enclosed with delicately perforated marble screens filled with translucent glass, so that a subdued filtered light invests the place. The actual tombs of Shah Jahan and Mumtaz Mahal are placed in a crypt exactly beneath the cenotaphs, of which they are an exact replica.

Like most Mughal mausoleums, the Taj Mahal is a garden tomb. The site selected for the mausoleum was the garden of Raja Jai Singh of Jaipur. The spacious garden is laid out in the *char bagh* style (rectangle divided into four equal parts), with a spacious marble platform at the centre. A row of fountains placed some feet from each other is carried from end to end with a beautiful walkway on both sides.

Above: *The 99 names of Allah on Mumtaz Mahal's tomb.*

Below: *Circular inlay motif on Shah Jahan's cenotaph.*

Centre: *The Taj Mahal on a clear morning. The pristine purity of the white marble makes the Taj the most enduringly beautiful monument in the world.*

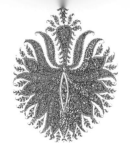

TRI-COLOUR LAMB SHASLIK
Kebab-e-Daryaee

PREPARATION: 1 HR. • COOKING TIME: 40 MIN. • SERVES: 4

Ingredients

Lamb, washed, cut into medium-sized pieces	750 gm / 26 oz
Ginger (*adrak*) juice	2 tbsp / 50 ml / 1¾ fl oz
Yoghurt (*dahi*), hung	1 cup / 260 gm / 9½ oz
Cinnamon (*dalchini*), 1″ stick	1
Cloves (*laung*)	6
Brown cardamom (*badi elaichi*)	2
Ghee	¼ cup / 55 gm / 1¾ oz
Black peppercorns (*sabut kali mirch*), crushed	1 tsp / 4 gm
Onions	3
Salt to taste	
Coriander (*dhaniya*) seeds, crushed	4 tbsp / 24 gm
Quail eggs, hard-boiled, shelled	20
Saffron (*kesar*), dissolved in 1 tbsp hot water	1 tsp
Beetroot (*chukander*) juice, mixed with 1 tbsp hot water	1 tsp

Method

1. Marinate the lamb with ginger juice and yoghurt.
2. Grind the cinnamon stick, cloves, brown cardamom seeds, and black peppercorns to a fine powder and keep aside.
3. Fry one sliced onion in ghee till golden brown. Add salt and crushed coriander seeds, stir. Add the marinated lamb and ½ cup of water, cook on low heat till the meat is tender and moisture evaporates. Sprinkle freshly ground spices, remove from heat and keep aside.
4. Cut the remaining onions into big pieces.
5. Take bamboo skewers and pierce the meat pieces, onion pieces, and eggs, alternately.
6. Colour the meat pieces with saffron, brush onion pieces with beetroot juice and cover the eggs with remaining marinade.
7. Grease a flat-bottom pan wide enough to hold the skewers. Arrange the skewers in the pan, sprinkle little water and cook on *dum* (see p. 20).

Shah Jahan and Jahangir feasting with Nur Jahan; Mughal, 18th century;
National Museum of India.

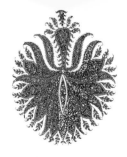

CHICKEN ROYAL
Murgh-e-Taaus

PREPARATION TIME: 1 HR. • COOKING TIME: 40 MIN. • SERVES: 4

Ingredients

Chicken, cut into 8 pieces	2 (750 gm / 26 oz each)
Yoghurt (*dahi*)	1½ cups / 335 gm / 11¾ oz
Ghee	½ cup / 110 gm / 3¼ oz
Green cardamom (*choti elaichi*)	4
Black cardamom (*badi elaichi*)	1
Cloves (*laung*)	6
Cinnamon (*dalchini*), 2″ stick	1
Onion, sliced	1
Ginger (*adrak*), chopped	1½ tbsp / 10¾ gm
Turmeric (*haldi*) powder	⅓ tsp
White pepper (*safed mirch*) powder	2 tsp / 10 gm
Poppy (*khus khus*) seed paste	2 tsp / 10 gm

Almonds (*badam*), blanched, ground	¼ cup / 60 gm / 2 oz
Sunflower seed (*chironji*) paste	¼ cup / 60 gm / 2 oz
Melon (*magaz*) seed paste	2 tsp / 10 gm
Cream	½ cup / 120 ml / 4 fl oz
Mace (*javitri*) powder	½ tsp / 2½ gm
Green cardamom powder	¼ tsp
Saffron (*kesar*), dissolved in rose water	¼ tsp
Pistachios (*pista*), blanched, cut into slivers	15
Pine nuts (*chilgoza*)	10
Walnuts (*akhrot*), halved	2

Method

1. Whisk the yoghurt in a bowl with salt. Marinate the chicken in this mixture for 30 minutes.
2. Heat the ghee in a pan; add whole spices and sauté on medium heat. Add onion and fry till golden brown. Add ginger and stir-fry. Add turmeric powder, white pepper powder, and ½ cup water to blend the spices; fry for a minute.
3. Add the chicken along with the marinade. Add 1 cup water, and bring the mixture to the boil on high heat. Lower heat and simmer until chicken is cooked.
4. Add poppy seed, almond, sunflower seed and melon seed pastes; bring to the boil and simmer until ghee surfaces. Add cream and mix well.
5. Sprinkle mace and green cardamom powders and saffron. Check seasoning and serve garnished with pistachios, walnuts, pine nuts, and walnuts.

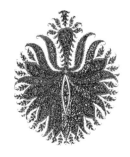

RICE AND LAMB PULAO
Yakhni Pulao

PREPARATION TIME: 1 HR. • COOKING TIME: 1 HR. • SERVES: 4

Ingredients

Lamb with bones	750 gm / 26 oz	Yoghurt (*dahi*)	1 cup / 225 gm / 8 oz
Rice	2½ cups / 500 gm / 1.1 lb	Garlic paste	2 tbsp / 36 gm / 1¼ oz
Garlic (*lasan*)	2 tbsp	Onions, sliced, fried and	
Coriander (*dhaniya*) seeds	1½ tbsp / 9 gm	ground to paste	1 cup / 170 gm / 5¾ oz
Cinnamon (*dalchini*), 1″ sticks	2	Black peppercorns (*sabut kali mirch*),	
Salt to taste		freshly ground	1 tsp / 4 gm
Cloves (*laung*)	8	Saffron (*kesar*)	1 tsp
Ghee	½ cup / 110 gm / 3¼ oz	Vetiver (*kewra*) essence	¼ tsp
Ginger (*adrak*) paste	2 tbsp / 36 gm / 1¼ oz	Green cardamom (*choti elaichi*), powdered	5

Method

1. Cook the lamb with garlic, coriander seeds, cinnamon stick, salt, and 1 cup water on low heat until soft and tender. Remove the pan from the heat and keep aside to cool.

2. Strain the stock and separate the lamb pieces. Temper the stock with 4 cloves and keep aside.

3. Heat the ghee in a pan; sauté the ginger paste. Add the lamb pieces, stir-fry. Add yoghurt and garlic paste. Continue to fry until the moisture evaporates. Add brown onion paste and mix well.

4. Add black pepper powder, saffron, vetiver essence, and half of the green cardamom powder. Add the stock, increase heat and bring to one boil. Lower heat and simmer.

5. Parboil the rice with enough water to cover. Add the remaining cloves and green cardamom powder. When the rice is parboiled and each grain is separate, spread the lamb mixture over the rice, seal the pan and cook on *dum* (see p. 20) for 5-7 minutes. Serve garnished with golden crisp fried onions.

ALMOND PISTACHIO BREAD
Naan-e-Nemat

PREPARATION TIME: 1 HR. 30 MIN. • COOKING TIME: 15 MIN. • SERVES: 4

Ingredients

Refined flour (*maida*)	2 cups / 250 gm / 9 oz	Almonds (*badam*),	
Salt to taste		blanched, peeled	¼ cup / 30 gm / 1 oz
Milk	½ cup / 120 ml / 4 fl oz	Pistachios (*pista*), blanched cut into	
Ghee	½ cup / 110 gm / 3¼ oz	fine slivers	¼ cup / 35 gm / 1¼ oz
Cream	1 tbsp / 15 ml	Raisins (*kishmish*),	
Yoghurt (*dahi*)	¼ cup / 55 gm / 1¾ oz	chopped	¼ cup / 35 gm / 1¼ oz
Saffron (*kesar*)	½ tsp	Saffron, dissolved in rose water	a pinch

Method

1. Sift the flour with salt in a bowl. Add milk and knead to make a soft dough.
2. Add 1 tbsp hot ghee and cream; knead and cover for 1 hour.
3. Mix the yoghurt with saffron and temper with 1 tsp ghee. Keep aside.
4. Uncover the dough, knead again with the yoghurt mixture, and divide it into 4 equal portions.
5. Dry roast the almonds and grind to powder.
6. On a working surface, sprinkle some refined flour and roll each portion into a round disc, apply ghee, sprinkle almond powder, pistachios and raisins. Bake the rotis in a preheated oven (180ºC / 350ºF) till golden. Remove and sprinkle saffron.

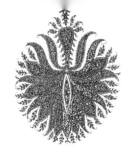

INDIAN BREAD PUDDING
Lauzeena

Ingredients

Bread loaf, one-day old, crusts removed	1	Milk	2 cups / 500 ml / 16 fl oz
Ghee	1 cup / 220 gm / 8 oz	Raisins (*kishmish*)	10 gm
Sugar	1 cup / 200 gm / 7 oz	Pistachio (*pista*) slivers	¼ cup / 35 gm / 1¼ oz
Saffron (*kesar*)	½ tsp	Almond (*badam*) slivers	¼ cup / 30 gm / 1 oz
Wholemilk fudge (*khoya*), crushed	1 cup / 100 gm / 3¼ oz	Saffron	a pinch
		Rose water (*gulab jal*)	¼ cup
		Silver leaves (*varq*)	4

Method

1. Cut each slice of bread into half. Fry the slices in hot ghee until brown. Remove and keep aside.
2. Mix 2 cups water with sugar and make sugar syrup of one-string consistency. Add saffron and mix well. Dip each slice of bread into the hot syrup, remove and keep on a tray.
3. Boil the milk till reduced to half. Add wholemilk fudge and mix well.
4. On a flat tray, pour ½ of the milk mixture, spread the bread slices carefully, and sprinkle raisins, pistachios, and almonds. Pour the remaining milk mixture and syrup on top of the bread. Bake for 10-12 minutes or until the mixture is dry. Remove and serve at room temperature.
5. Sprinkle saffron dissolved in rose water and serve decorated with silver leaves.

Aurangzeb spears an elephant; Mughal, 18th century;
British Library.

Aurangzeb
(1618-1707)

NAME	ABU MUZAFFAR MOHI-UD-DIN
TITLE	AURANGZEB ALAMGIR
BORN AT	DAHOB (INDIA)
DATE OF BIRTH	NOVEMBER 3, 1618
DATE OF CORONATION	JULY 22, 1658
ZODIAC SIGN	SCORPIO
DIED ON	MARCH 3, 1707
BURIED AT	AURANGABAD

Aurangzeb reading the Quran; Mughal, 18th century;
National Museum of India.

The last of the great Mughals, Aurangzeb, reigned longer than all his predecessors and heirs. He was one of the fatal figures of history who dominated all the events and overshadowed all the other personalities of his age, yet failed to secure the future of his own house. Aurangzeb, the third son of Shah Jahan, was born on November 3, 1618, when his father was serving as the viceroy of the Deccan. On his surrender as a rebel, he was conditioned to surrender his two sons, Dara and Aurangzeb, to his father as hostages. Till 1628 the prince remained under the care of Nur Jahan. When Shah Jahan ascended the throne, his sons were restored to him. At 16, Aurangzeb was given the command of 10,000 horses. In 1635, he was given his first field assignment of Bundela campaign. The following year, he was appointed the governor of Deccan, a post that he held for eight years, when he was abruptly dismissed but soon he regained the royal favour and was appointed governor of Gujarat. This glory was short lived and the relation between father and son soured badly. Aurangzeb was bitter and angry with his father and never forgave him.

As early as summer of 1658, on July 22, Aurangzeb held a coronation Durbar in the Shalimar Bagh outside Delhi, on the Karnal road, in order to strengthen the morale of his supporters for administrative reasons. He deferred the formal coronation to a later date. On June 5, 1659, he mounted the peacock throne in the Red Fort with splendid ceremonies and assumed the title of Alamgir (world conqueror). The festivities lasted for 14 weeks. The war of succession had thrown the machinery of the Mughal administration out of gear, consequently people were distressed and discontented. They were subjected to several taxes, legal and illegal. In order to alleviate their sufferings, Aurangzeb abolished as many as 80 taxes.

When Aurangzeb ascended the throne, he could hardly have imagined that he would spend more than half of his reign in the Deccan. He spent most of his time living in tents, enduring hardships, and waging wars. By the year 1690-91, Aurangzeb was at the height of his power. Nearly the whole of India was under his sway. He had succeeded in achieving what he had been struggling for. A glance at the map will show that Aurangzeb was Lord paramount of the whole of India, extending from Kashmir in the north to Cape Comorin in the south and from Kabul in the west to Chittagong in the east. The main framework of the government machinery under him was the same as under his predecessors. He tried to draw a line of demarcation between religion and politics, yet in practice he carried on the administration of his kingdom in accordance with the rules laid down in the Quran.

From there on, the Mughal dynasty began to crumble at an amazing speed. Many historians blame Aurangzeb and his destructive policies for eroding the common man's faith in the dynasty. However, this is by far an overstatement. Whatever the policies of Aurangzeb, he was very much the emperor till his dying day, in 1707. Though his policies did lead to resentment; the blame for the decline of the Mughals must definitely be shared.

If one agrees with the theory that after every golden period a decline must inevitably follow, then the disintegration of the Mughal empire becomes easy to explain. The golden period of the Mughals is said to be the reign of Shah Jahan. By the end of his reign, the signs of rot setting in were clear for all to see. The

golden rays, which seemed to be fading at the end of Shah Jahan's rule were brightened to a large extent by Aurangzeb in his initial years. But, the Deccan, wringed Aurangzeb the man, the king, the father, and the believer of all softer emotions and decorum. He simply lost his sense of balance. He alienated a sizeable portion of his subjects, allies and employees, and made unnecessary enemies, which cost his successors dearly. During his lifetime, he tried to put down rebellions all over his empire (the Marathas, the Sikhs, the Satnamis and the Rajputs) with one hand while trying to take Deccan by the other. However, it was like trying to douse the wild fire. Ultimately, it was these alternative power blocks that sped up the fall of the Mughals. Not to mention the foreign powers that were already among those present: the British stretching their legs in Calcutta, the Portuguese in Goa, and the French testing waters in the south.

Aurangzeb celebrated his succession in the ordinary way of princes, especially of princes who had succeeded after civil strife to the throne. He reduced the taxes. To comfort the people and alleviate their distress, the Emperor gave orders for the remission of the *Rahdari* (toll), which was collected on every highway (*guzar*), frontier and ferry, and brought in a large sum to the revenue. He affected economy everywhere. He reduced the expenses of the court drastically and maintained a well-organized department called the *Bait-ul-Maal* or God's treasury. Justice was rigorously administered and the Emperor himself sat in the Diwan-e-Khas on every Wednesday and with the help of his law officer attended the cases. He was an eminent educationist. For the widespread diffusion of education, he established learning centres in all-important cities and opened madrasas in small towns.

Aurangzeb's political pre-occupation left him but little leisure to indulge in artistic fancy. He did make some addition to the existing architecture. Among the most remarkable is Moti Masjid in Red Fort and Badshahi Masjid at Lahore. Quite unlike his predecessors, Aurangzeb did not patronize music and painting. He regarded both music and painting as sinful, while his taste in literature was rusticated to work of theology and poetry of devotional character. Yet the glorious reign of this simple king was not without its beautiful gardens. The garden of Roshan Ara Begun in Delhi and Pinjore Gardens at Chandigarh deserve mention. He also founded the city of Aurangabad. Aurangabad was rich and populous and through it passed major trade routes.

It is a fact that he did not maintain a big harem. The only story of his infatuation with a concubine of his maternal aunt's husband, the beautiful Zainabadi, from Zainabad, in Burhanpur, finds reference in historical records.

The only indulgence of the Emperor was love for the pleasures of the table. He once wrote to his son, 'I remember the savour of your *khichdi* and biryani during the winter, I wanted to have from you Suleman, who cooks biryani, but you did not allow him to serve me as my cook, if you happen to find a pupil of his skill in the art of cooking you will send him to me, the desire for eating has not left me entirely.' He was a vegetarian and did not like exotic dishes of meat prepared in the royal kitchen. He loved *qubooli* and enjoyed this preparation. Like his ancestors, Aurangzeb had a passion for fruits, especially for mangoes, and there are numerous references to mangoes in his letters. He was a simple and religious emperor hence the practice of serving food in gold and silver dishes was forbidden by him.

Wine was not a taboo in the Mughal society, except in the reign of Aurangzeb who never drank it except once when by irony of fate succumbed to the temptation at the hands of a beautiful slave girl, Zainabadi, who tried to test his infatuation for her.

It is impossible to under rate the character and achievements of Aurangzeb, he was simple and unassuming in his private life and magnificent in public appearances. He was, indeed, a triumph of character. He did lack the physical strength and exuberant vitality of the Mughals, but he did not lack the Mughal courage. In his youth, he did enjoy hunting and had built a monument to commemorate his hunting of two fighting antelopes in two shots. In his old age, he referred to hunting as the business of idle persons.

The majestic and the mystique of the Mughals ended with Aurangzeb's death. Aurangzeb died in the Deccan, in 1707, and was buried at a place called Khuldabad, which lies on the Aurangabad-Allora road. The simple mud grave did not cost more than fourteen and a half rupees, the amount he usually earned from sewing prayer caps or writing pages from the Holy Quran. On his grave he asked for nothing but the open sky and the fragrant Rehan shrub.

Aurangzeb's wife, Begum Rabia Durrani, was buried in Aurangabad in the *Bibi ka Maqbra*, built by Hasan Azam Shah who tried to imitate the Taj Mahal in a simple way.

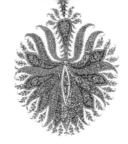

BROKEN WHEAT AND LENTIL PATTIES
Kebab-e-Burghul

PREPARATION TIME: 1 HR. 30 MIN. • COOKING TIME: 15 MIN. • MAKES: 20

Ingredients

Burghul or Broken wheat (*dalia*), soaked overnight	½ cup / 100 gm / 3¼ oz
Lentil (*masoor dal*), washed	½ cup / 100 gm / 3¼ oz
Semolina (*suji*)	3 tsp
Black peppercorns (*sabut kali mirch*), freshly ground	1 tsp / 4 gm
Salt to taste	
Onion, chopped	1
Green coriander (*hara dhaniya*), chopped	¼ cup / 15 gm
Lemon (*nimbu*) juice	1 tsp / 5 ml
Olive oil	½ tbsp / 7½ ml
Vegetable oil for frying	

Method

1. Drain the broken wheat and cook until soft. Cool and grind to a smooth paste.
2. Cook the lentil in just enough water (approx. 2 cups) until soft.
3. In a bowl, add semolina, broken wheat paste, cooked lentil, black pepper powder, and salt; mix well to form a smooth dough.
4. Add onion, green coriander, and lemon juice; knead again. Add olive oil and knead until the oil is well incorporated.
5. Divide the mixture into 20 equal portions and shape into patties. Shallow-fry on a griddle until golden and crisp on both sides.
6. Serve hot with mint chutney.

Note: Burghul is crushed wheat which has been boiled, dried in the sun and then ground. It can be obtained from food stores. If not available cracked wheat can be used.

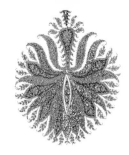

STUFFED EGGPLANT TOPPED WITH YOGHURT SAUCE
Boorani Badanjaan

PREPARATION TIME: 30 MIN. • COOKING TIME: 30-40 MIN. • SERVES: 4

Ingredients

Lamb mince	500 gm / 1.1 lb
Eggplants (*baingan*), large, top removed, slit into	
4 pieces keeping bottom intact, pricked	
and soaked in cold water, drained, pat dried	2
Ghee	½ cup / 110 gm / 3¼ oz
Onions, sliced	1½ cups / 250 gm / 9 oz
Lentil (*masoor dal*), soaked in cold water	
for ½ hour, drained	½ cup / 100 gm / 3¼ oz
Cinnamon (*dalchini*) powder	1 tsp / 5 gm
Clove (*laung*) powder	1 tsp / 5 gm
Black peppercorns (*sabut kali mirch*)	½ tsp / 2 gm

Brown cardamom (*badi elaichi*)	1
Ginger (*adrak*), chopped	1 tbsp / 7½ gm
Coriander (*dhaniya*) seeds, crushed	1 tbsp / 6 gm
Salt to taste	
Mint (*pudina*), chopped	1 tbsp / 4 gm
Yoghurt (*dahi*), hung,	
whipped	½ cup / 130 gm / 4¼ oz
Roasted rice powder	1 tbsp
Garlic (*lasan*) paste	1 tbsp / 18 gm
Saffron (*kesar*), dissolved in water	¼ tsp
Walnuts (*akhrot*), chopped	1 tbsp

Method

1. Heat half the ghee in a pan; fry the onions until golden. Add the lamb mince and stir-fry for 3-4 minutes.

2. Add lentil, half of the spices (reserve some for garnishing), ginger, crushed coriander, salt, and ½ cup water; cover and simmer on low heat until the lentil and minced meat are cooked.

3. Fill the eggplants with the above mixture (reserve some for later use). Tie a thread around to secure the filling.

4. In another pan, spread the reserved filling; arrange the eggplants on it and pour hot ghee over and around them. Garnish with mint and remaining spices. Seal the pan and cook on *dum* (see p. 20).

5. In a serving dish, spread the filling mixture and place the eggplants over it. Mix yoghurt with roasted rice powder and garlic paste. Temper with clove. Pour yoghurt evenly over the eggplants. Serve garnished with saffron and walnuts.

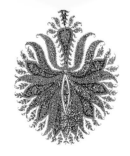

RICE AND BENGAL GRAM PULAO
Qubooli

PREPARATION TIME: 30 MIN. • COOKING TIME: 45 MIN. • SERVES: 4

Ingredients

Bengal gram (*chana dal*), soaked in water for 20 minutes	1¼ cups / 250 gm / 9 oz
Rice, long grain, soaked in water for 20 minutes	2½ cups / 500 gm / 1.1 lb
Vegetable oil	⅔ cup / 145 ml / 4¾ fl oz
Onions, finely sliced	3
Ginger (*adrak*) paste	1 tsp / 6 gm
Garlic (*lasan*) paste	1 tsp / 6 gm
Turmeric (*haldi*) powder	¼ tsp
Yoghurt (*dahi*)	1 cup / 225 gm / 8 oz
Green chillies	4
Red chilli powder	1 tsp / 5 gm
Dried apricots (*khoobani*), destoned, soaked for 15 minutes, drained	¼ cup
Dried plums (*alubukhara*), destoned, soaked for 15 minutes, drained	¼ cup
Dried prunes, destoned, soaked for 15 minutes, drained	¼ cup
Cloves (*laung*)	4
Cinnamon (*dalchini*), ½" stick	1
Brown cardamom (*badi elaichi*)	3
Black cumin (*shah jeera*) seeds	½ tsp / 1¼ gm
Black peppercorns (*sabut kali mirch*)	½ tsp / 2 gm
Saffron (*kesar*), dissolved in rose water	1 tsp
Mint (*pudina*) leaves, fresh, chopped	2 tbsp / 8 gm
Green coriander (*hara dhaniya*), fresh, chopped	¼ cup / 15 gm
Lemon (*nimbu*) juice	¼ cup
Milk	⅓ cup / 80 ml / 2¾ fl oz
Ghee	2 tbsp / 24 gm

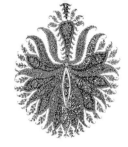

Method

1. Boil the Bengal gram in enough water to cover with salt and a pinch of turmeric powder till tender.
2. Parboil the rice with salt. Drain the water and spread the rice on a flat dish, cover and keep aside.
3. Heat the oil in a pan; fry the onions till golden brown, remove half and keep aside. Add ginger and garlic pastes, stir-fry till golden. Add turmeric powder and stir. Add yoghurt, stir-fry. Add 2 deseeded green chillies.
4. Add the Bengal gram and red chilli powder; cook for 2 minutes. Add the dried apricots, plums and prunes; cover the pan and simmer.
5. Grind the whole spices to a fine powder.
6. Brush the bottom of a heavy-bottomed pan with oil. Spread half of the parboiled rice and saffron, and then spread the dal mixture over it. Sprinkle the ground spice powder, half the mint, green coriander, green chillies, and lemon juice. Cover with remaining rice and saffron. Sprinkle milk, fried onions, remaining mint, green coriander, and green chillies. Make another layer. Dot the rice with ghee, pour milk on the sides, cover the pan and cook on *dum* (see p. 20).
7. Serve garnished with fried onion slices and almonds.

Illuminated Manuscripts

An illuminated manuscript is a manuscript in which the text is supplemented by the addition of decoration, such as decorated initials, borders and miniature illustrations. In the strictest definition of the term, an illuminated manuscript only refers to manuscripts decorated with gold or silver. Early Mughal rulers brought with them a passionate love and demand for illustrated books and manuscripts.

Producing of illuminated manuscript required the cooperation of calligraphers, painters, preparaters for various accessories, such as colour grinders, gold workers, leather workers, book binders, and many more. The books to be copied and illustrated were often very long, and could be done with the help of these craftsmen.

Among the many innovations introduced by the Mughal, perhaps, the most important was the concept of *karkhana* or workshop. The object of *karkhana* was to bring diverse artist together under one roof and foster better communication among them and experiment new ideas and techniques, this contributed to the visual revaluation of the Mughal.

The Mughal dynasty ruled India from 1526-1707 and each emperor produced beautifully illustrated manuscripts during his reign. Babur wrote the *Baburnama* and started the practice of saving records of his reign. Gulbadan Begum, his daughter, who recorded the events of Humayun's time with beautiful illustrations followed this.

The art of illustrating manuscripts developed with time and during the period of Emperor Akbar it reached its zenith. The artifact produced in the royal court of Akbar, the *Hamzanama*, included 1400 huge folios, arranged in 14 boxes each kept in a large box.

Manuscript of the Windsor Padshahnama *of Abdula Hamid Lahori, 1656-7.*

The *Akbarnama*, which literally means 'history of Akbar', is a biographical account of Akbar, the third Mughal emperor, written in Persian. This is the most famous illustrated manuscript of the Mughal period. It includes vivid and detailed descriptions of his life and time. The book was commissioned by Akbar, and written by Abul Fazl, one of the nine jewels of Akbar's royal court.

Jahangir, the fourth Mughal emperor, was a lover of beauty, be it that of an artifact created by human hands or that observed in nature, the work of god. His memoirs, commonly known as *Tuzuk-i-Jahangiri* or *Jahangirnama*, are as much an album of his aesthetic experiences as a chronicle of his reign. With his keen sensibility, these experiences were a permanent source of joy for him. Nature and beauty were preserved through the brush of his artists.

Some opportunities occur not once in a lifetime, nor once in a century, but just once. The *Padshahnamah* manuscript is not only an artistic achievement, but also contains important historical events. There are 44 illustrations in the book painted by prominent court painters. Abdul Hamid Lahori's *Padshahnamah* is a voluminous work containing 1662 printed pages, each page of 22 lines. The *Padshahnamah* shows a more thoughtful approach to perspective, they are not simple generic illustrations of 'the hunt' or 'the feast' and so on; rather, they are accurate, almost empirical records, which,

The Shamsa *(image of the sun) is a divine light, which god directly transfers to kings, without the assistance of men; and the kings are fond of external splendour, because they consider it an image of the Divine glory.*

like press photographs today could be retrieved from an archive to check. The text is written in Persian and each page is stamped with an owner's seal. With the coming of Aurangzeb the art of painting declined and the art developed by his ancestors died a natural death.

BOTTLE GOURD KOFTAS IN CREAMY GRAVY
Kofta Angoori

PREPARATION TIME: 50-55 MIN. • COOKING TIME: 20-25 MIN. • SERVES: 4

Ingredients

Bottle gourd (*lauki*), peeled, grated	500 gm / 1.1 lb
Salt to taste	
Gram flour (*besan*)	²/₃ cup / 100 gm / 3¼ oz
Green chillies, deseeded, finely chopped	2
Ginger (*adrak*), finely chopped	1 tbsp / 7½ gm
Salt to taste	
White pepper (*safed mirch*) powder	½ tsp / 2½ gm
Cottage cheese (*paneer*)	½ cup / 50 gm / 1¾ oz
Wholemilk fudge (*khoya*), crushed	¼ cup / 25 gm
Spinach (*palak*) juice	1 tbsp / 15 ml
Pistachios (*pista*), blanched, pounded	½ cup / 70 gm / 2¼ oz
Silver leaves (*varq*)	
Vegetable oil for frying	

For the gravy:

Ghee	¼ cup / 55 gm / 1¾ oz
Green cardamom (*choti elaichi*)	6
Cloves (*laung*)	4
Bay leaves (*tej patta*)	2
Onions, boiled, ground	100 gm / 3¼ oz
Garlic (*lasan*) paste	½ tsp / 3 gm
Ginger (*adrak*) paste	1 tsp / 6 gm
Coriander (*dhaniya*) powder	1 tbsp / 7½ gm
Poppy seed (*khus khus*) paste	1 tsp / 5 gm
Cashew nut (*kaju*) paste	2 tbsp / 30 gm / 1 oz
White pepper powder	½ tsp / 2½ gm
Tomato purée	2 tbsp / 30 ml / 1 fl oz
Salt to taste	
Cream	1 cup / 240 ml / 8 fl oz
Green cardamom powder	½ tsp / 2½ gm
Mace (*javitri*), powdered	¼ tsp

Method

1. Boil the bottle gourd with a pinch of salt until soft. Drain and squeeze gently to remove excess moisture.
2. In a bowl, mix gram flour, green chillies, ginger, salt, white pepper, cottage cheese, half of the wholemilk fudge, and spinach juice. Add bottle gourd and mix well.
3. Divide the mixture into 20 equal portions and shape into balls. Flatten each ball and place a pistachio in the centre; reshape again.
4. Deep-fry the balls to golden brown and keep aside. Cover each kofta with silver leaf.
5. **For the gravy**, heat the ghee in a pan; add green cardamom, cloves, and bay leaves, stir and add onion paste. Sauté on medium heat until translucent. Add garlic and ginger pastes and sauté. When the onion becomes light pink, add poppy seed and cashew nut pastes; fry for 2-3 minutes. Add white pepper powder, salt, tomato purée, and 1 cup water to blend the spices; stir-fry until the oil surfaces. Simmer on low heat.
6. Add cream and remaining wholemilk fudge; blend well and simmer for 2 minutes. Sprinkle freshly ground green cardamom and mace powders, stir and remove from heat.
7. Float the koftas in the gravy while serving.

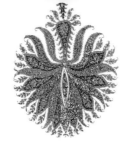

RICH CREAMY BLACK GRAM
Dal Alamgiri

PREPARATION TIME: 30 MIN. • COOKING TIME: 45 MIN. • SERVES: 4

Ingredients

Black gram (*dhuli urad dal*), washed, soaked overnight, drained	3 cups / 600 gm / 22 oz	Red chilli powder	½ tsp / 2½ gm
Black peppercorns (*sabut kali mirch*)	1 tsp / 4 gm	Milk	2 cups / 500 ml / 16 fl oz
Cinnamon (*dalchini*), 1″ stick	1	Cream	4 tbsp / 60 ml / 2 fl oz
Cloves (*laung*)	5	Salt to taste	
Brown cardamom (*badi elaichi*)	2	Yoghurt (*dahi*), whisked	¼ cup / 55 gm / 1¾ oz
Ghee	2 tbsp / 24 gm	Saffron (*kesar*), dissolved in milk	1 tsp
Onions, medium-sized, sliced	2	Mint (*pudina*), fresh, chopped	1 tbsp / 4 gm
Coriander (*dhaniya*) powder	2 tsp / 10 gm	Ginger (*adrak*), chopped	2 tsp

Method

1. Cook the black gram on high heat. After just one boil remove, drain and keep aside.
2. Grind black peppercorns, cinnamon stick, cloves, and brown cardamom to a fine powder.
3. Heat the ghee in a pan; fry the onions till crisp and golden brown, remove half and keep aside. Add dal, coriander powder, and red chilli powder; cook for 5 minutes.
4. Add milk, cream, salt, and the powdered spices. Cover and cook on low heat for about 20 minutes or until the dal is cooked but not mashed, if dal is not cooked as desired, little water can be added.
5. Strain the yoghurt and pour into the cooked dal and blend. Sprinkle the saffron mixture; cover the pan and simmer for 5 minutes.
6. Serve garnished with mint, ginger, and fried onions.

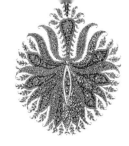

BARLEY AND CHICK PEA DELIGHT

Aash-i-Jau

PREPARATION TIME: 30 MIN. • COOKING TIME: 1 HR. 30 MIN. • SERVES: 4

Ingredients

Chick peas (*kabuli chana*), soaked overnight, boiled	¾ cup / 150 gm / 5 oz
Barley, soaked overnight	½ cup
Ghee	1 cup / 220 gm / 8 oz
Onion, cut into slices	1
Cloves (*laung*)	4
Brown cardamom (*badi elaichi*)	2
Cinnamon (*dalchini*), 1″ sticks	2
Lamb, medium-sized pieces	500 gm / 1.1 lb
Black peppercorns (*sabut kali mirch*), crushed	1 tbsp / 4 gm
Mint (*pudina*), fresh, chopped	1 tsp
Green coriander (*hara dhaniya*), chopped	1 tbsp / 4 gm
Salt to taste	
Lemon (*nimbu*) juice	1 tsp / 5 ml
Saffron (*kesar*)	¼ tsp

Method

1. Boil the barley once and drain the water. Add fresh water, boil again and drain. Repeat this process three times. Add enough water to cook barley, bring to the boil and simmer until barley is white and tender.

2. Heat ½ cup ghee in a pan; sauté the onion till golden brown. Add 2 cloves, brown cardamom, 1 cinnamon stick, lamb, and 2 cups water. Cook on medium heat till lamb is tender and soft. Remove from heat.

3. Separate the lamb pieces from the stock and keep aside. Strain the liquid and then temper with 2 cloves and 1 cinnamon stick. Repeat the process three times. Bring the mixture to the boil. Lower heat, add barley and chick pea to the pot; mix well and simmer.

4. Mash the reserved lamb pieces and add to the barley mixture. Heat the remaining ghee; temper the barley mixture with black pepper. Add mint, green coriander, salt, and lemon juice, mix well.

5. Transfer the mixture to a serving bowl, pour hot ghee and serve with a dash of saffron.

COTTAGE CHEESE BREAD
Naan-e-Paneer

PREPARATION TIME: 30 MIN. • COOKING TIME: 20 MIN. • SERVES: 4

Ingredients

Cottage cheese (*paneer*), grated	1 cup / 100 gm / 3¼ oz	Ghee	½ cup / 110 gm / 3¼ oz
Refined flour (*maida*)	2 cups / 250 gm / 9 oz	Milk	½ cup / 125 ml / 4 fl oz
Salt to taste		Cottage cheese, cut into thin slices	8
		Yoghurt (*dahi*), whisked	2 tbsp / 30 gm / 1 oz

Method

1. Sieve the flour and salt together in a bowl. Add cottage cheese, ghee, and milk; knead to make a smooth dough.

2. Divide the dough into 8 equal portions and roll out round discs of 5-6″ diameter. On each disc, place one slice of cottage cheese, and apply whisked yoghurt over the cottage cheese slices.

3. Place the bread on a greased baking tray and bake in a preheated oven at 180°C / 350°F for 10 minutes or cook covered on a griddle (*tawa*). Repeat till all are done.

RICE AND MANGO DESSERT
Biranj-e-Amba

PREPARATION TIME: 45 MIN. • COOKING TIME: 45 MIN. • SERVES: 4

Ingredients

Mango (*aam*), pulp	2 cups	Saffron (*kesar*)	½ tsp
Rice	1½ cups / 300 gm / 11 oz	Ghee	2 tbsp / 24 gm
Milk	2 cups / 500 ml / 16 fl oz	Mango, sliced for garnishing	
Sugar	½ cup / 100 gm / 3¼ oz	Almond (*badam*) slivers	2 tbsp
Cream, whipped	½ cup / 120 ml / 4 fl oz	Pistachio (*pista*) slivers	2 tbsp

Method

1. Warm the milk, add sugar and cook on low heat for ½ hour. Remove and cool.
2. Pass the mango pulp through a muslin cloth. Add cream and saffron; mix well. Keep aside.
3. Boil the rice with a pinch of salt and ½ tbsp ghee; drain. Add the thickened milk and cook on medium heat, stirring continuously for 10 minutes. Remove and cool.
4. Grease a pan, arrange alternate layers of rice, and mango mixture ending with rice. Dot the rice with remaining ghee. Cover the pan tightly and cook on *dum* (see p. 20).
5. Serve garnished with mango slices, almond and pistachio slivers.

Colour portrait of Bahadur Shah Zafar made for Theophilus John Metcalfe in 1844.

Bahadur Shah Zafar
(1775-1862)

NAME	BAHADUR SHAH
TITLE	ZAFAR
BORN AT	DELHI
DATE OF BIRTH	OCTOBER 24, 1775
DATE OF CORONATION	SEPTEMBER 18, 1838
ZODIAC SIGN	SCORPIO
DIED ON	NOVEMBER 7, 1862
BURIED AT	RANGOON (YANGOON)

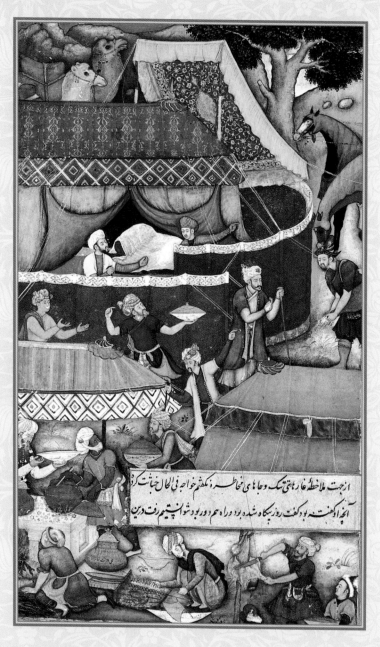

Food being prepared in the Royal camp; Mughal, 18th century;
National Museum of India.

The last Mughal king, Bahadur Shah, better known as Bahadur Shah Zafar, was born in 1775 in Delhi. He was the son of Akbar Shah from his Hindu wife, Lalbai. Bahadur Shah, after the death of his father, was placed on the throne in 1838 when he was little over 60 years of age. He was last in the lineage of Mughal emperors who ruled over India for about 300 years. Bahadur Shah Zafar, like his predecessors, was a weak ruler who came to throne when the British domination over India was strengthening and the Mughal rule was nearing its end. The British had curtailed the power and privileges of the Mughal rulers to such an extent that by the time of Bahadur Shah Zafar, the Mughal rule was confined to the Red Fort. Bahadur Shah Zafar was obliged to live on British pension, while the reigns of real power lay in the hands of the East India Company, who had expanded their power domination throughout the country. Thus the Emperor was left to spend his time in creative exercises than administration.

As mentioned, the last Mughal emperor, Bahadur Shah Zafar, was the king of Delhi in name only. The real governance was in the hands of Britishers. Bahadur Shah received a pension of Rs 12 lakhs per annum. Besides, an annual income of Rs 36,000 was received from royal estates. Out of the pension, Rs 5 lakhs was his personal allowance and the rest 7 lakhs was for the heir apparent and other princes. A major portion of the king's income was spent on giving salaries to his servants, whose number was more than 400.

However, the great 'War of Independence' took place during his reign in 1857. The freedom fighters, Muslim and Hindu soldiers of the East India Company reposed faith on the leadership of Bahadur Shah and they nominated him as the supreme leader. The British, after the initial setback, crushed the movement. They overthrew and arrested Bahadur Shah from Humayun's tomb, in Delhi, where he was hiding with his sons and a grandson. Captain Hudson killed his sons, Mirza Mughal and Khizar Sultan, and grandson, Abu Bakr. Their severed heads were brought before him. Bahadur Shah Zafar himself was tried for treachery. He was exiled to Rangoon (now Yangoon), Burma (now Myanmar), in 1858 where he lived his last five years. This formally ended the Mughal dynasty that started with Babur in 1526. Bahadur Shah Zafar was kept in a shed attached to the bungalow of a junior British officer, along with his wife, Zeenat Mahal, and granddaughter, Raunaq Zamani.

Bahadur Shah died a sad and broken man. A plaque on the wall, written in Urdu, English and Burmese languages, narrates the story, 'Bahadur Shah, ex-king of Delhi, died at Rangoon, November 7, 1862 and was buried near this spot.' Another line says, 'Zeenat Mahal, wife of Bahadur Shah, who died on July 17, 1886, was also buried near this spot.'

Of course, the British kept no sign of his grave; possibly fearing an uprising based on nationalist sentiments throughout India. Later, while digging for the foundation of a memorial hall on the site in 1991, the real mausoleum was found. The mausoleum, a must visit for every Indian, Pakistani, and Bangladeshi, in the capital of Burma, includes a room for the tombs of his wife and granddaughter with a prayer hall in front. Bahadur Shah Zafar's tomb covered with a green satin cloth is placed in an underground chamber.

A big painting of Bahadur Shah Zafar, placed in front of the prayer hall greets visitors to the campus that contain the line, 'The last emperor of India, Bahadur

Shah Zafar's Dargah.' Interestingly, the great Indian freedom fighter, Netaji Subhas Chandra Bose, who led the Indian National Army against the British, gave the famous call 'Delhi Chalo' (March to Delhi) in 1942 to Indians thirsting for freedom from this historic place.

Every Indian along with the Pakistanis and Bangladeshis respect him as the last emperor of undivided India, but people of Burma worship him as a saint. His grave attracts devotees from different places with different religious faiths. In fact, Bahadur Shah lived as an emperor and died as a *pir* (a holy man) in a foreign land. The common people of Burma believe that Bahadur Shah, who ruled India centuries ago, is a saint-scholar. They come to his Dargah and pray in front of his tomb convinced that their wishes would be fulfilled.

The last Mughal emperor of India, who reigned from 1837 to 1858, was a poet, musician, and calligrapher, more an aesthete than a political leader. During his reign, Urdu poetry flourished and reached its zenith. He himself was a prolific poet and an accomplished calligrapher. He had acquired his poetic taste from his grandfather and father who were also poets. He passed most of his time in the company of poets and writers and was the author of *Four Diwans*. Love and mysticism were his favourite subjects that found expression in his poetry. Most of his poetry is full of pain and sorrow owing to the distress and degradation he had to face at the hands of the British. A scholar of Sufism, a poet, and a ghazal writer, Bahadur Shah penned his own epitaph before his death. The ruler turned saint wrote, *Kitna hai badnaseeb Zafar, dafn ke liye do gaz zamin bhi na mili ku-e-yaar mein.* (How unlucky is Zafar! He couldn't find even two yards of earth for burial in his beloved land/country). He was a great patron of poetry and literary work and some of the most eminent and famous Urdu poets like Mirza Ghalib, Zauq, Momin, and Daagh adorned his court.

Besides poetry, Bahadur Shah was also interested in food, though he was not a gourmet but his *dastarkhwan* was the richest and most varied amongst the Mughal emperors. His table had Turkish, Persian, Afghani, and

Bahadur Shah Zafar, Delhi, 1850.

Indian flavours of different regions, and also some of the European confectionaries. A cursory glance at the preparations, which adorned his table, is a vital proof of his fondness for food.

Persian and Central Asian cuisine travelling in the camp kitchens of the conquers made its ways into northern India creating the flavours and aroma which form the elaborate culinary art of this region. Food was then interwoven into the fabric not only mere substance but as part of the cosmic cycle in accordance with the Unani medicine. Rejuvenated by the Mughal influence, diverse texture, smell, colour, and taste enriched by spices and dried fruits became a celebration of life.

Kebabs of venison and castrated fowl, fried partridges and quail, roasted duck, lamb and fish soaked in sour yoghurt and cooked with condiments, potatoes, lamb's chest cooked on slow fire throughout the night, whole cauliflower cooked in goat soup, fried peas and eggplants served with sauce, pulaos of lamb and chicken, biryani (the queen of delicacies), chapattis, *paratha*, *nans*, *kulchas*, and the delicious royal *baqar khani* (made of milk, butter and walnuts), besides dozens of sweet dishes, custard, *kheer* (cooked with rice, almond, pistachio, mango, carrot and gram), etc. were served on the dining table of Bahadur Shah. He himself had invented several delicacies, for instance, *halwa* of bitter gourd, *mirchon ka dulma*, and a chutney called *rahat jani* with *besan ki roti*. Bahadur Shah was 83 and did not have strong digestion to enjoy the delicacies. He derived pleasure by feeding others present on the *khasa*. It is said that Bahadur Shah Zafar started his meal with the soup of quail. Once the British Resident of Delhi sent him a gift of 15 choicest mangoes, which he ate in one go and was taken ill. When he recovered a little, he indulged in the luxury of food again and was confined to bed for four months.

Bahadur Shah Zafar was also very fond of *moong dal* (green gram) which was cooked with great care and was called *dal shah pasand*. Once the emperor sent this preparation to the famous poet of his court, Mirza Ghalib, who wrote a quadren on this dish and presented it to the emperor. At the Royal *dastarkhwan*, Zeenat Mahal would be seated next to him along with the nobles remembered by him.

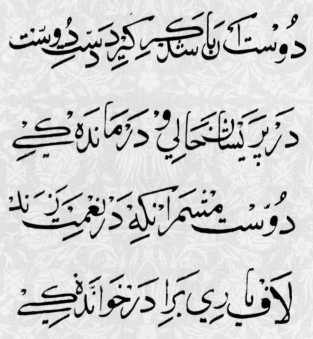

Autograph of Bahadur Shah Zafar of Delhi;
April 29th, 1844.

133

A prince being entertained in the harem; National Museum of India.

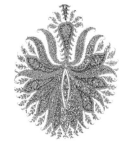

KEBABS COOKED IN A PAN
Pateeli Kebab

PREPARATION TIME: 1 HR. 30 MIN. • COOKING TIME: 30 MIN. • SERVES: 6

Ingredients

Chicken legs, skinned, deboned, flatten with steak pounder	6 (100 gm / 3¼ oz each)	Raisins (kishmish), soaked in water for 15-20 minutes	3 tbsp
Yoghurt (dahi), hung	½ cup / 130 gm / 4¼ oz	Pistachios (pista), blanched, pounded	3 tbsp
Garlic (lasan) paste	½ tsp / 3 gm	Apricots (khoobani), destoned, roughly chopped	6-8
Ginger (adrak) paste	½ tsp / 3 gm	Saffron (kesar), dissolved in 1 tbsp milk	½ tsp
Salt to taste			
White pepper (safed mirch) powder	½ tsp / 2½ gm	Ghee	3 tbsp / 45 gm / 1½ oz
Lemon (nimbu) juice	3 tbsp / 45 ml / 1½ fl oz	Silver leaves (varq)	4
Almonds (badam), blanched, pounded	3 tbsp		

Method

1. Whisk the yoghurt along with garlic and ginger pastes, salt, white pepper powder, and lemon juice.
2. Rub the yoghurt marinade evenly on both sides of the chicken legs and arrange on a tray, not overlapping each other. If any extra marinade is left spread over the chicken legs. Marinate for an hour.
3. Mix all the dried fruits thoroughly together. Divide the mixture into 6 equal portions.
4. Take each chicken leg, drizzle some saffron and place a portion of the dried fruit mixture on the broader side and roll. Tie each roll with banana leaf thread or with a twine.
5. Grease a thick-bottomed *pateeli* (pan) with ghee and arrange the chicken rolls. Cook on high heat, turning once. Baste occasionally with ghee. When the rolls are light brown on all sides, reduce heat and finish on *dum* (see p. 20).
6. Serve decorated with silver leaves.

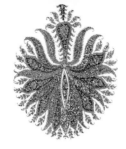

LAMB MINCE WITH PISTACHIOS
Piston Ka Keema

PREPARATION TIME: 10 MIN. • COOKING TIME: 30 MIN. • SERVES: 4

Ingredients

Lamb mince	750 gm / 26 oz	Salt to taste	
Pistachios (*pista*), blanched, pounded	1 cup / 140 gm / 5 oz	Garlic pod, whole, soaked in water	1
		Cloves (*laung*)	3
Ghee	1 cup / 220 gm / 8 oz	Green cardamom (*choti elaichi*)	2
Onions, sliced	½ cup / 185 gm / 2¾ oz	Cinnamon (*dalchini*), ½" stick	1
Garlic (*lasan*) paste	1 tsp / 6 gm	Bay leaf (*tej patta*)	1
Ginger (*adrak*) paste	1 tsp / 6 gm	Black peppercorns	
Red chilli powder	½ tsp / 2½ gm	(*sabut kali mirch*)	¼ tsp
Coriander (*dhaniya*) powder	½ tsp / 2½ gm	Silver leaves (*varq*)	2

Method

1. Heat the ghee in a pan; add the onions and fry till golden brown. Remove and reserve half.

2. Add garlic and ginger pastes, red chilli powder, coriander powder, and salt with ½ cup water and sauté on low heat until the ghee starts separating. Add lamb mince, mix and fry, sprinkling garlic water (not permitting lamb mince to stick to the pan). The mince should get cooked with the process of sautéing with garlic water. It will take approximately 15-20 minutes.

3. In the meantime, grind all the whole spices to a fine powder.

4. When the lamb mince is cooked and the ghee has surfaced, check seasoning. Sprinkle freshly ground spice powder. Add pistachios and simmer for 2 minutes. Remove from heat.

5. Serve decorated with silver leaves.

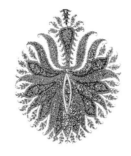

STUFFED FISH SLOW COOKED TO PERFECTION
Machli Dum Pukht

PREPARATION TIME: 45 MIN. • COOKING TIME: 40 MIN. • SERVES: 4

Ingredients

Sole fish, skinned, washed	I kg / 2.2 lb	Sunflower seeds (*chironji*)	2 tbsp / 20 gm
Gram flour (*besan*)	²/₃ cup / 100 gm / 3¼ oz	Coconut (*nariyal*), dessicated	2 tbsp
Yoghurt (*dahi*)	I cup / 225 gm / 8 oz	Pistachios (*pista*), blanched, peeled,	
Juice of lemon (*nimbu*)	I	finely chopped	2 tbsp
Salt		Mace (*javitri*)	2 blades
Ginger (*adrak*)	I tbsp / 7½ gm	Green cardamom (*choti elaichi*)	4
Garlic (*lasan*)	2 tbsp / 15 gm	Cloves (*laung*)	5
Almonds (*badam*),		Black peppercorns (*sabut kali mirch*)	4
peeled	¼ cup / 30 gm / I oz	Saffron (*kesar*), dissolved in I tsp	
Poppy (*khus khus*) seeds, roasted	2 tbsp / 20 gm	rose water	I tsp

Method

1. Slit the fish lengthwise on the belly side. Clean and wash with cold water. Rub the fish with gram flour. Dilute yoghurt with I cup water and leave the fish in it to soak for 15-20 minutes. Remove and wash with cold water.

2. Rub the fish with lemon juice and salt. Keep aside for 15 minutes.

3. Grind ginger, garlic, almonds, poppy seeds, sunflower seeds, coconut, and pistachios along with the whole spices to a fine paste. Keep aside.

4. Apply saffron mixture evenly on the marinated fish. Stuff the fish with the above paste.

5. Place the fish along with the marinade in a greased flat pan large enough to hold the whole fish. Secure with banana leaf and cook on low heat for 30-40 minutes or until the fish is cooked.

6. Serve hot garnished with lemon wedges.

LAMB, VEGETABLE AND LENTIL SOUP

Shorba Malghuba

PREPARATION TIME: 1 HR. 30 MIN. • COOKING TIME: 10 MIN. • SERVES: 4

Ingredients

Lamb, cut into medium-sized pieces	320 gm / 11½ oz
Onion, cut into quarter	1
Brown cardamom (*badi elaichi*)	2
Cloves (*laung*)	6
Cinnamon (*dalchini*), 1" stick	1
Black peppercorns (*sabut kali mirch*), crushed	1 tsp / 4 gm
Black cumin (*shah jeera*) seeds	½ tsp / 1¼ gm
Turnip (*shalgam*), peeled, cut into small pieces	1
Carrots (*gajar*), peeled, cut into cubes	2
Spinach (*palak*), washed, chopped	½ bunch
Ginger (*adrak*), chopped	2 tsp
Split red gram (*arhar dal*), soaked for 10 minutes	¼ cup / 50 gm / 1¾ oz
Green gram (*moong dal*), soaked for 10 minutes	¼ cup / 50 gm / 1¾ oz
Bengal gram (*chana dal*), soaked for 10 minutes	¼ cup / 50 gm / 1¾ oz
Rice, soaked for 10 minutes	¼ cup / 50 gm / 1¾ oz
Salt to taste	
Lemon (*nimbu*) juice	2 tbsp / 30 ml / 1 fl oz
Saffron (*kesar*)	¼ tsp
Cream	¼ cup / 60 gm / 2 fl oz
Black pepper, for garnishing	

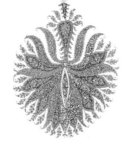

Method

1. Cook the lamb on low heat with onion, brown cardamom, 4 cloves, cinnamon stick, crushed black peppercorns, black cumin seeds, and 4 cups water till lamb is soft and tender. Remove from heat and keep aside to cool. Remove the bones, mash the meat and reserve. Strain the stock and reserve.

2. In a separate pan, heat 1 tbsp ghee; add all the vegetables and stir-fry. Cook on low heat adding 1 cup water. When the vegetables are soft and cooked, remove from heat. Pass though a sieve and add to the reserved stock.

3. Cook all the dals and rice together in the stock. When cooked well, remove from heat. When cool, pass though a sieve or purée to make a smooth paste.

4. Mix the mashed meat into the dal purée; ensure that the consistency is soup-like. Add little boiled water, if necessary to correct the consistency. Bring to the boil and then simmer for 2-3 minutes.

5. Heat 1 tbsp ghee in a pan to smoking; add 2 cloves. When they start spluttering pour into the soup, cover and simmer for another 2-3 minutes.

6. Season the soup with salt and lemon juice.

7. Dissolve saffron in cream and add to the prepared dish.

8. Serve sprinkled with freshly ground black pepper.

LAYERED LAMB RICE ENRICHED WITH DRIED FRUITS
Mutanjan Pulao

PREPARATION TIME: 1 HR. 30 MIN. • COOKING TIME: 15 MIN. • SERVES: 4

Ingredients

Rice	2½ cups / 500 gm / 1.1 lb	Almonds (*badam*), blanched,	
Lamb with bones	200 gm / 7 oz	cut into slivers	10
Onion, sliced	1	Pistachios (*pista*), blanched,	
Ginger (*adrak*), chopped	1 tbsp / 7½ gm	cut into slivers	10
Coriander (*dhaniya*) powder	1 tbsp / 7½ gm	Raisins (*kishmish*), soaked	2 tbsp
Salt	a pinch	Dried dates (*chuhara*), soaked	5
Cloves (*laung*)	8	Milk	2 cups / 500 ml / 16 fl oz
Sugar	1½ cups / 300 gm / 11 oz	Saffron (*kesar*)	1 tsp
Juice of lemons (*nimbu*)	2	Rose water (*gulab jal*)	1 tsp
Ghee	½ cup / 110 gm / 3¼ oz	Gold leaves (*varq*)	2

Method

1. Cook the lamb with onion, ginger, coriander powder, salt, and 2 cups water. When the lamb is tender, remove and keep aside to cool. Separate the lamb from the stock. Strain the liquid, add the lamb and temper it with cloves.

2. Add sugar (reserve 1 tbsp) and juice of 1½ lemons to the stock. Bring to the boil.

3. Heat the ghee in a separate pan; fry the dried fruits. Add 1 tbsp sugar and milk. Cook for 5 minutes.

4. Parboil the rice in water with the remaining lemon juice.

5. Grease the bottom of a thick-bottomed pan; spread the lamb mixture, sprinkle saffron, cover with half of the fried dried fruits, and top with parboiled rice. Sprinkle rose water, cover and cook on *dum* (see p. 20) for 8-10 minutes.

6. Serve garnished with the remaining dried fruits and gold leaves.

UNLEAVENED GRAM FLOUR BREAD
Besani Roti

PREPARATION TIME: 20 MIN. • COOKING TIME: 20-25 MIN. • SERVES: 6-8

Ingredients

Gram flour (*besan*)	3 cups / 450 gm / 1 lb	Yoghurt (*dahi*), hung	¾ cup / 200 gm / 7 oz
Onions, chopped	¾ cup / 130 gm / 4¼ oz	Carom seeds (*ajwain*)	½ tsp
Ghee	1 cup / 220 gm / 8 oz	Saffron (*kesar*)	1 tsp
Salt to taste		Green coriander (*hara dhaniya*), chopped	2 tbsp / 8 gm
Milk	1 cup / 240 ml / 8 fl oz	Green chillies, chopped	2-3

Method

1. Sift the gram flour into a bowl.
2. Squeeze the onions with hand to remove excess water.
3. In a bowl, mix gram flour, onions, ghee (reserve 2 tbsp for greasing the griddle), and salt; add milk and knead to a hard dough. Leave aside for 10 minutes.
4. Gradually, add yoghurt, carom seeds, saffron, green coriander, and green chillies; knead again to a smooth dough.
5. Divide the mixture into 12 equal portions and roll out discs of 5″ diameter. (Little thicker than ordinary chapatti.)
6. Grease the griddle (*tawa*) with ghee. Place the disc and cook adding little ghee on the sides. Remove when brown on both sides.

Bahadur Shah Zafar, the last ruler of the Mughal dynasty, before his departure for exile in Rangoon. This is the only photograph ever taken of a Mughal emperor.

VERMICELLI DESSERT

Sheer Khurma

PREPARATION TIME: 15 MIN. • COOKING TIME: 30 MIN. • SERVES: 4

Ingredients

Vermicelli (*sevain*)	50 gm / 1¾ oz	Sunflower seeds (*chironji*),	
Ghee	3 tbsp / 45 gm / 1½ oz	washed, cleaned	2 tbsp / 20 gm
Pistachio (*pista*) slivers	2 tbsp	Green cardamom (*choti elaichi*)	
Almond (*badam*) slivers	2 tbsp	seeds	1 tsp
Raisins (*kishmish*), soaked in water	1 tbsp	Sugar	½ cup / 100 gm / 3¼ oz
Dried dates (*chuhara*)	1 tbsp	Saffron (*kesar*)	¼ tsp
Milk, fresh	8 cups / 2 lt / 64 fl oz	Silver leaf (*varq*)	1

Method

1. Heat 2 tbsp ghee in a pan; lightly fry the dried fruits, separately. Remove and keep aside.
2. Heat the milk on low heat, stirring frequently, and cook until the milk is reduced to half.
3. Heat the remaining ghee in a pan; add the sunflower seeds and green cardamom seeds and stir-fry. Add the fried dried fruits and milk, cook on medium heat for 5 minutes. Remove from heat and keep aside to cool.
4. Add sugar and vermicelli, mix well and simmer for 5 minutes.
5. Sprinkle saffron and serve at room temperature garnished with silver leaf.

Index